THE SELECTED POEMS
OF ROBERT DESNOS

ACKNOWLEDGMENTS

I would like to thank Genviève Martin, Christine Cotaz-Bertholet, and
Laure-Anne Bosselaar for their patient readings and suggestions. I am also
very grateful for the Massachusetts Artists' Foundation fellowship which
enabled me to complete this work.

— C.F.

THE SELECTED POEMS
OF ROBERT DESNOS

Translated by Carolyn Forché and William Kulik
Edited with an Introduction by William Kulik

THE ECCO PRESS
New York

The Ecco Press
26 West 17th Street
New York, NY 10011
Published simultaneously in Canada by
Penguin Books Canada Ltd., Ontario
Printed in the United States of America
Designed by Jody Hanson
FIRST EDITION

Grateful acknowledgment is made to Les Editions de Minuit for permission to translate the poem, "Le veilleur du Pont-au-Change."

Translations by William Kulik appear on pages 1–48, 90–124, and 165–180.

Translations by Carolyn Forché appear on pages 49–89 and 125–164.

Library of Congress Cataloging-in-Publication Data

Desnos, Robert, 1900–1945.
    [Poems. English. Selections]
    The selected poems of Robert Desnos
translated by Carolyn Forché and William Kulik.—1st ed.
       p.   cm.—(Ecco's modern European poetry series)
    1. Desnos, Robert, 1900–1945—Translations, English.
I. Forché, Carolyn, II. Kulik, William T., III. Title. IV. Series.
PQ2607.E75A25 1991   841'.912–dc20   90-3165   CIP
ISBN 0-88001-261-7

The text of this book is set in Perpetua

Frontispiece photo of Robert Desnos sleeping courtesy of Jean Loup Charmet.

CONTENTS

. . . a translation issues from the original—not so much from its life as from its afterlife.

—Walter Benjamin

Behind the cathedral of Notre Dame and across the quais, there is a black iron gate opening to a white stairwell that leads into the bank of the Seine. Descending, one enters rooms hollowed from the earth: rounded, austere, and as white as the palpable silence of this place. The windows of the rooms are barred against the flow of the river, whose waters seem invisibly held back. To the right, there is a tunnel, and at its entrance a black grave marker inscribed: *"ici repose un déporté inconnu."* "Here lies the unknown deported." Along the tunnel walls, two hundred thousand tiny lights flicker; at the end a single light burns like a star in the surrounding darkness. This is the "Memorial to the Deportees," the two hundred thousand Jews deported from France to the camps during the *Shoah.* It was here that I first encountered the poetry of Robert Desnos, chiseled into a wall. Desnos, a member of the Resistance, had been among those deportees.

    I was young and in Paris for the first time. I opened my notebook and copied the lines out:

J'ai rêvé tellement fort de tol
J'ai tellement marché, tellement parlé,
Tellement aimé ton ombre
Qu'il ne me reste plus rien de toi,
Il me reste d'être l'ombre parmi les ombres
D'être cent fois plus ombre que l'ombre
D'être l'ombre qui viendra et reviendra
        dans ta vie ensoleillée

    The name, Robert Desnos, was obliterated when the notebook was left carelessly open to the rain. I knew only that I had been moved by the poem, which remained for years mysterious to me, poignant and moving, lyrical and elegiac, when read as a message to the deported.

    In 1986 I returned to Paris again, this time to await the birth of my son. My husband and I were living at 11 rue Schoelcher, in an atelier overlooking the cemetery of Montparnasse. In an armoire, I found a small collection of books, among them the Seghers Edition of Robert Desnos. During that rainy March, I sat at a bread table pulled to the window and passed the last days of my pregnancy translating this poet. Toward the end of the book and my confinement, I was startled to recognize the lines from the wall. I had found Robert Desnos, and these lines, under the title *Le Dernier Poeme* in my Seghers, were thought to have been with the poet when he died of typhoid fever at Terezin. I translated them:

> I have dreamed so strongly of you
> I have walked so much, talked so much
> So much I have loved your shadow
> That there now remains for me nothing more of you,
> It remains with me to be a shadow among shadows
> To be a hundred times darker than the darkness
> To be the shadow that will come and come again
> > into your sun blessed life.

I have since learned that the poem carved into the memorial is thought to be spurious—a translation from Czech back into French of lines taken from another longer Desnos poem bearing the title *"J'ai rêvé tellement fort de toi."* I prefer to imagine that Desnos might have retrieved these lines from his wounded memory and spoken them again during the delirium of typhus; that they were perhaps taken down by the young Czech medical student who attended the dying poet, or by the young nurse, then made into Czech to be shared with others in the open-air hospital village that Terezin had become. The only support I have for this theory is that it seems plausible to my heart.

It was this fragment, this translation of a translation, that first brought me to the work of Robert Desnos. In this, I take comfort from Walter Benjamin's meditations on the translator's work: that we labor in a field of broken chards, and retrieving each fragment, we attempt to piece together a work that will never resemble the original. As a restored vessel will never again hold water, my English versions of Desnos's poems will never hold the music and resonance of the French. But Benjamin counsels us that "no translation would be possible if in its ultimate essence it strove for likeness to the original. . . . Unlike a work of literature, translation does not find itself in the center of the language forest but on the outside facing the wooded ridge; it calls into it without entering, aiming at that single spot where the echo is able to give, in its own language, the reverberation of the work in the alien one." My task, as I began to perceive it, was not to translate Desnos's French into my English, but to translate my English into the poetry of Desnos.

It was a matter of translating one epoch of human apprehension into another, one mind into another, of allowing myself to be inhabited by the spirit of a poet distanced by time, history, extremity, and by a youth spent in the wilderness of an experimental project I had never undertaken on my own. It was rather like the task of conjuring a ghost. So it seemed that often, in struggling within the rather closed linguistic cosmology of this poet, I found myself estranged from my own being. It was necessary to wait in meditative expectancy for one of Desnos's peculiar visitations, when a line or passage would arise as if from the caverns of a memory not my own.

The poems of his Surrealist period, and the trace of Surrealism that remained in his later work, proved the most intransigent. According to Breton, Surrealists had "restricted themselves to the prompting of being, speaking from the darkness of the wings." As a Surrealist, Desnos became a poet at dream-speed, writing out of self-induced trance, as the inscriber of automatic texts that offer a frisson of new meaning in their original tongue, a frisson difficult to bear across the bridge of translation. How many times did I scribble in the margins of the earliest versions: *what does this mean?*—only to surrender later to an equivalent that seemed acceptable to my ghost. Of necessity, I attempted such writing, tutored by Aragon's *"Il n'y a pas de pensées hors des mots."* "There are no thoughts outside of words," and Tzara's *"La pensée se fait dans la bouche."* "Thought takes place in the mouth." Most resistant to my efforts were Desnos's many puns, homonyms, syntactical inversions, neologisms, internal rhymes, tongue twisters, and sound plays. Often an entire poem would arrive in English without yielding to me its metonymic secrets.

During the year I lived in Paris, the language that began as the indecipherable music of the street, the café, the train, became the language of my daily life and, finally, of my waking thought. So I could bring to the poems my little knowledge that the green flowering windows of Desnos's pharmacy were green neon crosses, and that coins actually do "ring" on the bar tops of bistros, because the bars are of cheap zinc. My French friends, however, had to help me to understand that the marigold is thought of as "the flower of worry," that the wound in Christ's side is sometimes described as a "rose," that the lines "drawn on the compass face" were also a "rose," and that *émoi* is more than emotion, more than passion: it is agitated, excited feeling for which there is no single word in English. Simple. But without these explanations, I would surely have remained lost.

It took three years for me to complete my share of the work in this volume. During that time, Desnos became for me a poetic mentor. In his "Reflections on Poetry," translated by Michael Benedict in New York City, June 6, 1971, he wrote: "Poetry can be this or it can be that. It ought not be restricted to being necessarily this or that . . . except perhaps for being both delirious and lucid. . . . It seems to me that

beyond Surrealism there is a mysterious something that has yet
to be isolated; beyond automatism there is intent, beyond poetry
there is the poem, beyond passive poetry there is deliberate poetry,
beyond liberated poetry there is the liberated poet . . . try now
and then, young poets, my beloved friends, to see that you are not
yet really free."

For his participation in the French Resistance, Desnos was arrested
by the Gestapo and interrogated under torture. He was sent to the camp
at Compiègne, then to Auschwitz, Buchenwald, and Floha. In April of
1945, he was force-marched to Terezin, Czechoslovakia, where he died
shortly after the camp was liberated by Russian troops.

This past May, I visited Terezin. We drove the black Teplice road
under a white sky, past the cut fields, the tarpaulin-covered hay ricks, the
petrochemical plant spewing black smoke. Poppies afflicted the hay fields
with wounding brilliance. The people were harvesting cauliflower then
from the gardens near Terezin. As we neared the town and its fortress-
prison the silence of the deportees' memorial returned: infinite and
impenetrable. It was Sunday. The town, once a ghetto for one hundred
and sixty thousand, is inhabited again, but the streets are oddly empty.
We watched a boy, blank-eyed, pedaling a bicycle back and forth with a
naked, broken doll in its basket. The windows of Terezin were lace
curtained, but the walls were rotting away, and many buildings were
boarded and vacant. We drove the streets under flowering chestnuts and
circled the empty park. At the entrance to the prison, a woman stood
holding a bouquet of leeks wrapped in paper. Two Czech soldiers strolled
through what had once been the women's compound. Doors swung in the
wind. Swallows dipped into the prison yard and rose again, their cries
slicing into the silence without leaving a mark. We walked the cold,
swept-clean barracks, ran our fingers over the gray washbasins, the long
trestle tables, the tiered bunks. We found the sign: *Arbeit macht frei*. We
found the little drawings and paintings made by the children of Terezin:
colorful houses and trees, children and animals, birds, flowers, butterflies.
We picked forget-me-nots and left them near a symbolic gravestone. This
is where Desnos died. Somewhere here, carved into a wall, are the words:
"Ici mourut Le Poète et Résistant Francais Robert Desnos 18 juin 1945." As a
prayer, I said the little spurious poem that had first opened his life and
work to me. It is in the spirit of this poem that I offer my versions of his
work in English, that he may be known by American readers and so live
again, one among the many who perished, the soul of a poet who gave his
heart to the world in France.

—Carolyn Forché
July 13, 1990

At the time of his arrest by the Gestapo, on February 22, 1944, Robert Desnos was forty-three years old, the author of thousands of lines of poetry, novels, and a full-length study of the erotic in literature, plus scores of reviews and appreciations of film, records, art, and literature, a number of scenarios and songs, one very famous radio play, and in the neighborhood of three thousand commercials. In addition, he was entirely or in part responsible for the writing, direction, and production of dozens of radio broadcasts, the most famous of them called *La clef des songes* (*The Key to Dreams*), a weekly show in which he read and interpreted dreams sent to him by listeners. Though the war brought the series to an end, a journal entry dated February 11, 1944, shows him planning a classification of dreams, into which he could fit any example with ease. The journal also shows him considering other projects, including a collection of his work in which the freely associated poems of his twenties would sit side by side with his most recent, formal ones. And a letter to his wife from Buchenwald speaks of his plan for "a love story in an entirely new genre." A fellow inmate says that a box filled with Desnos's camp writings did not survive. Neither did Desnos.

This intensely productive man, a passionate dreamer and collector of all kinds of cultural artifacts who scoffed at the usual distinctions between high and low culture, wrote for a living as well as for "art." This lover of wine, women, cats, and popular song used radio to bring Mozart and Beaumarchais and Sisley to the workingman—without debasing the former or patronizing the latter—and was delighted to spend a whole night listening to records of Satie and Sophie Tucker, Bach followed by Varèse by Chevalier. And this man, so exceptionally talented in so many areas, was as a child what we today call gifted. Writing, painting, recording his dreams, able to focus with intensity only on what mattered to him, he spent his childhood and adolescence struggling for the right to be free, leaving home at sixteen to gain, as he said later in life, that freedom his parents denied him.[1]

A modern middle-class parent, attentive to—in fact hovering over—every phase of his child's development, would have recognized early on his son's precocity and encouraged it, perhaps with art lessons, subliminal tapes, alternative schools, other forms of what we call "enrichment." But not Lucien Desnos, who himself had followed the well-marked path from provincial obscurity to modest but solid success as sales agent for poultry and game at the famed Les Halles market and a twenty-year stint as deputy mayor of his district, achieving these ends by means of the traditional bourgeois virtues of thrift, hard work, piety, and patriotism, virtues he tried to drum into his son. Dreamy Robert was not interested. Instead of playing the good little boy, he gave himself to the mysterious charms of his ancient neighborhood, the Quartier St-Merri, feeding his imagination with the tales surrounding the alchemist Nicholas Flamel, a resident of the same neighborhood half a millennium earlier, entranced by the ancient buildings and alleyways as much as by the daily marvels of bustling commercial life, probably half "here" and half "there" most of the time, and not caring very much which was which.

His father persevered, without much success. A photo taken in 1908 at Robert's first holy communion indicates that some religious training was imposed. But there is little evidence, outside of Desnos's lifelong anticlericalism (which included clerics of all religions), of any religious passion. He was always passionate about literature, exclusively. He could barely stomach math. Even the First World War seems to have escaped his notice. The teacher's common criticism. "Does not work up to potential" was leveled at him time and again. When he graduated from Lycée Turgot in 1916, he said good-bye to school and left home soon after, avid for the absolute freedom his nature seems to have demanded.

Free of his family, he wrote, painted, recorded his dreams, and made new friends: anarchists, Dadaists, believers, like himself, in the right to develop according to the laws of one's own being. He fell into the easy café life, living on the fringes, sharing food and sometimes girls. By 1919 he even had a job he liked. Then two years of military service in Morocco intervened, during which time he fretted at being cut off from the Parisian literary scene. Returning in 1922 and feeling very much out of the flow, he begged his friend Benjamin Peret to introduce him to André Breton, leader of the newest movement: Surrealism.

His entrance into the Surrealist coterie dovetailed with the beginning of the *epoque des sommeils,* the trancelike "sleeps" the members were encouraged to fall into in order to speak and write "automatically," transmitting directly to the daylight world the pure products of the unconscious. This psychic automatism was one of the keys, Breton felt, to the world revolution Surrealism sought: to show the possibility of discovering whole buried universes in each of us, worlds made up of repressed desire that, though apparently inchoate, were obedient to their own laws; and thus to help create this new consciousness of his buried possibilities—man by man until it became universal—and an irresistible will that would ultimately force the creation of a new society, one that would fulfill, not deny, the true needs of mankind.

Perfect for the rebel Desnos, for the young man who'd been recording his dreams since childhood, who could drop off to sleep in a crowded café[2] and speak fluently, poetically, to the astonishment and envy—and sometimes the suspicion—of the others. With this ability to

erase the boundary between sleep and waking, Desnos quickly moved to
the center of the group, becoming the protégé of Breton, who praised him
as the perfect example of the new man, brave explorer of unknown seas,
one who was "a thousand times more revolutionary than the revolution,"
one who "spoke Surrealist." And a man with nearly endless wit, as the
one hundred fifty spoonerist aphorisms of *Rrose Selavy* (1923) demonstrate.
Untranslatable—like the title itself, "Eros, c'est la vie"—they virtually
exhaust the possibilities of punning in French. To read them is like
listening to an hour of Groucho Marx playing on "ice water" and "eyes
water" or Groucho and Chico doing the "viaduct, vy-a-chicken" routine
or, maybe even more to the point, like hearing the twisted aphorism
"Never leave a tern unstoned." Similarly, in *Language cuit*—language
"cooked" or "done"—a product of the same period, nothing is allowed to
impede the wit, the high-level language game Desnos plays to the hilt. It is
a mixed bag of concrete poems, poems based on homonym punning, and a
number that play games with grammar and parts of speech: using
redundant modifiers and tautologies, having nouns and verbs change roles.
All of these good Surrealist experiments were designed to kick bourgeois
logic in the teeth, to show that language is not only for signifying, that, in
fact, a lot of what we signify is as nonsensical as these poems, that
language may, in fact, have laws of its own—and those who are willing to
take the plunge will discover them, as Desnos had.

In addition to being the foremost sleep-talker and a prolific
contributor to Surrealist publications, the quick-tempered young poet,
passionate in the defense of his beliefs, was at the forefront of the group's
public demonstrations, which were staged, much like those of the Dadaists
before them, to publicize their ideas and often to provoke and then punish
the opposition. Though he was of medium build and not athletic, Desnos
was quick with his fists, even if he was sure to get the worst of it.

By 1925 the energy of the movement had peaked, and changes were
soon to come that would reduce his importance to it. Breton had begun to
realize, as much from personal experience as from badgering by his
Marxist friends, that discovering psychic truths and publicizing them
would not bring about the revolution. Besides, he feared for the sanity of
those who, like Desnos, dove relentlessly to the bottom of things. So he
began to stress the need to adhere to a set of principles so close to those
of the Marxists that it was just a matter of time until Breton and his inner
circle—Eluard, Unik, and Aragon—joined the Communist party. At the
same time, he called an end to the sleep sessions, a decision whose weight
fell most heavily on Desnos, as his strength within the movement had been
his reckless, unfettered self-searching and self-expression. His nature—
intuitive, emotional, nonrational—could never be bridled, so eventually he
drifted to the fringes of the group, which came to be scorned as the

"literary wing," always suspect and forever coaxed to return to the new center.

Though nominally a Surrealist, Desnos would from now on follow his own path, which led in 1926 to a card in the journalists' union, a job with *Le Soir* (and later, other papers), and deepened conflict with Breton. Desnos loved the ease and the camaraderie with other journalists, so different from the seriousness he was accustomed to among the Surrealists. And he loved the freedom to write as he pleased about favorite subjects: film, art, music—especially recorded music. Breton, meanwhile, chided his departure from the intellectual rigor of the revolutionary path and thought Desnos deluded himself with the notion that the "bosses" would ever allow real freedom. The more attached to journalism Desnos became, the greater the distance between them grew so that their public denunciations of each other in 1929 merely sealed the fate that had long since been determined by their opposed natures.

In 1926 Desnos published his first collection of poems, *C'est les bottes des sept lieues cette phrase 'Je me vois'* (*It's the Seven League Boots That Phrase 'I See Myself'*). They are fine examples of the "arbitrary fragments"—Breton's "poetry imposed"—welling up from that subterranean source where "that one great poem was being elaborated," as Desnos was to say of his twenties' aesthetic. Perhaps the general tone of paranoia that characterizes the work is the result of too much diving to the depths of that source. The poems are set in landscapes of a mind that sees threats everywhere: threats to poetry, to the poet himself, to freedom, to love; from natural forces such as sharks and tidal waves; from poison-mixing chefs and mysterious concierges. Death stalks the poet in the guise of a white prince and the "postman of subtraction" who brings him the announcement of his end. He is even attacked by the tools of his trade. Ultimately, he is hopeful, as the wit of the last lines of "The Great Days of the Poet" suggests. And it is a species of wit not far removed from *Rrose Selavy* that inhabits these poems and works against too serious a reading of them. It is the commonplace transformed: "wipe your hands before praying," "Let them keep me in booze my whole death long/And leave me in war." Sometimes it's a line with the pith of a gnomic utterance: "If I like trains it's no doubt because they go faster than funerals." But the power of these poems is in the irrational mystery of their juxtaposed images, which create that "lightning-filled night" Breton called the objective of Surrealist poetry; that spark leaping the gap between the images imposed upon the poet who is in touch with his unconscious, who trusts in their "supreme reality." Of course, as with all poetry of this type, the reader must make the associative leap. And such poetry always runs the risk of inviting too-free associations or degenerating into nonsense, however highbrow. Desnos may have been aware of the possibility of this charge—or was

making the charge himself—when he spoke of many of his poems of this
period as "verbal fog."

By the time *C'est les bottes des sept lieues* was published, Desnos had
fallen desperately in love with Yvonne George, a music-hall singer whose
songs, he said, constantly expressed the sorrows of love and "the
intolerable absence of powerful emotion (*la pathetique*) in our lives." His
unanswered love for her was so strong it became an obsession and for
some time the only inspiration of his poetry, resulting in two collections
quintessentially Surrealistic. In them an atmosphere of *le merveilleux*—the
juxtaposition of the exotic and the ordinary, "the fabulous taken for
granted"—is created, and dream and waking reality become
indistinguishable. *À la mystérieuse* (*To the Mysterious Woman*), published in
1926, contains seven poems that read like love letters to the woman he
can't have in the flesh, though her presence haunts him night and day. She
is a phantom who becomes more real to him than she ever could be "in
reality." In "The Sorrows of Love," he identifies her with the miseries her
absence creates in him but calls them "dear" and "necessary." They are
"demanding muses"—inspirations his art requires. On the other hand, in
"If You Only Knew," a long meditation on her elusiveness, he plays with
the notion that he controls her; that though she won't yield to him in the
flesh, she does in the poem, as he says "through my will to possess your
illusion." And in "Sleep Spaces" we travel with the "I" following his
"you" through a succession of wonderful landscapes whose existence he
owes to her presence "at the depths of my dreams stirring up a mind full
of metamorphoses." Again, she is simultaneously subject and inspiration,
belonging to him in the substance of and for the duration of the poem, a
testament to the primacy of imagination in Desnos's life and work. It is
the same man, writing of the power of the female voice, who declares "It
is enough for me to hear one single word uttered by an invisible woman to
evoke her from head to toe with perhaps greater reality than in her
earthly appearance." And it's he who says that love and freedom can be
reconciled only in the poem.

The poems of *Les Ténèbres* (*Darkness*), published in 1927, the other
collection inspired by the singing star who claimed she was Nerval's
daughter, take place at midnight or in twilight or firelight, in the distant
past or the mythical present where anything can happen, even the most
astonishing adventures. In the keynote poem, "The Voice of Robert
Desnos," the poet, though master of his poetic universe, is unable to
attract the one thing he wants most: his love, who takes many forms. In
"Identity of Images" she is coal, amorphous and ubiquitous as carbon, the
perfect correlative for the elemental force of the mysterious woman. She is
also the swimmer, the mermaid, the star. He is the anchored boat whose
line she can cut at any time, boat endangered by reefs and storms, which

she, "queen of catastrophes," is mistress of; and he is the grass, the ivy, the edelweiss on the mountainside, withering if she wills it. These poems may be, as Breton called them, narcissistic, and the world he creates may be a solipsist's. But what a world! Of fabulous creatures, incredible metamorphoses, unbelievable actions: heads of hair and crystal dresses speaking, mines snoring, amorous sphinxes leaving the marks of their talons on waxed staircases. The poems are a *Grimm's* of Desnos's psyche, their logic the logic of dreams. Much as when reading *C'est les bottes des sept lieues,* we need to give ourselves to the leaps created by the juxtaposition of groups of words that, as Breton says, "create their own solidarity," so in reading *Les Ténèbres* we must, like children once more, listening to fairy tales, allow these movies of the mind to wash over us, to soak us. As they echo from poem to poem, the images begin to resonate with their own meaning within this closed universe. The coal, the cork, the schist, the sponge; mother-of-pearl, diamond, crystal, rainbow; and seagull, jellyfish, butterfly, all ultimately become familiar to us, even if we are never certain of their meaning, which must have been palpable to Desnos, who once said "I believe in the material reality of the imagination" and who tells us directly at the end of a poem to "Dream accept dreaming it's the poem of the new day."

By 1928 Yvonne George was in a Swiss sanatorium dying of tuberculosis. Though he felt as strongly about her as ever, Desnos went on with his café nights. These were high times for him. He knew everyone in the artistic world of polyglot Paris: Stein, Picasso, Hemingway, André Masson, Vallejo, Rivera, Dubuffet. He wrote constantly, poems and articles, day and night; he went to Havana for a congress of the Latin-American press and fed his love of music with the sounds and rhythms of the Caribbean. And he began to spend a lot of time partying with the painter Foujita and his beautiful, flirtatious wife, Youki, who drew crowds of admiring men wherever she went as a result of the popularity of her husband's paintings of her naked. Though Desnos was a loyal and generous friend to both the Foujitas, it's clear he was moved by her beauty and by her temperament, which, like his own, created great highs and deep lows. Their party went on for the better part of two years, until the money ran out. Youki grew restless for the nightlife, while Foujita was glad for the chance to stay home and paint. They fought, while Desnos tried to negotiate, pleading one side, then the other. Hoping they'd forget their differences, he took them on a drinking tour of Burgundy. And, pressing his finances to the limit, he rented them an apartment he thought would please Youki, where they lived until, as the story goes, the day Foujita went out for a pack of cigarettes and never came back, writing Desnos later to tell him to take care of Youki, writing Youki to tell her she'd be better off in loyal Robert's care.

It took Desnos the better part of two more years to convince Youki of that, during which time she came and went as she pleased—and with whom she pleased—which often drove poor Desnos to the brink. But he was determined to have her. To make money for her—the journalism had dried up—he took a ludicrous job as manager of an apartment building. Having been drummed out of the Surrealist corps at last by an exasperated Breton chastising the prodigal for his individualism and for failing to adhere to a few simple directives (such as joining the CP), Desnos responded with his own denunciation, declaring that Surrealism had "fallen into the public domain," which is where, after 1932, he was to spend his talent and energy as "one of [radio's] most productive slogan writers."

Between the publication in 1930 of his collected poems and the appearance in 1934 of the sixteen poems of Les sans cou, Desnos published no others, though he wrote many, a number of which were for Youki's eyes only. Many are about love; some apparently personal, others merely conventional. She must have been especially flattered by the ones that salute her as the mermaid, powerful and content in her invented world, since she got one tattooed on her thigh. But she's also "Lou the naughty" in the delightful "Lou the Shark Lady," whose final lines are like a coda of their early years.

And there are new themes and new attitudes—new, more direct expressions. An introspective mood appears, for example, in "Awakenings," with its vision of a self barely departed but already losing its reality; while joy in the purely physical spills over the borders of such poems as "Low Tide" and "The Second Song of the Marigold," an expression that will intensify in lyrics of the later thirties and early forties: "Coming Harvests," "Song for the Beautiful Season," "Coming Down Hillsides in Spring," and many others. As he settled into life with the beautiful Youki, holding down a regular job and entering middle age, a need for greater directness, a passionate clarity in the expression of the old truths gripped him—not to mention a turning outward toward others, an immense sympathy that found an outlet in what have come to be called the "fraternal poems" of Les sans cou, especially "Mid-way," an evocation of the marvelous events and the "dark thoughts" that occur at precisely the middle of one's life; "Swim," "Men," "Comrades," and "To the Headless," where the rousing voice that identifies with the misery of the masses is first heard; a voice that will be heard again in his great Resistance poems: "The Watchman of the Pont-au-Change," "The Legacy," and "This Heart That Hated War." Brought to life by Hitler and the depression, the old anarchist's new political concerns are deepened by the war in Spain—witness "Fire"—and the certainty that war with fascism was inevitable, even welcome.

But in 1932 things could hardly have been better for Desnos. His old friend Paul Deharme, a pioneer in French broadcasting, hired him at Radio Paris to handle publicity and advertising for the station. Shortly afterward, another old friend, Armand Salacrou, got him a contract to write commercials for a cosmetics firm. It was this writing, which he later characterized as "the almost mathematical but still intuitive work of adapting words to music," that saved his poetic career, which he felt had suffered complete burnout, especially after the "purge" he gave his intellect in 1936, when he undertook to write a poem every day of the year, tired or not, inspired or not. What he learned that year was the "mechanical demand" of form: "in the rhythm, in the necessity of assonance, and of primitive forms such as rhymed tercets," the finest examples of which are the clear, simple, but tightly controlled masterpieces of this period "June 10, 1936" and "Men on Earth."

Radio was to do even more for him than reorient his thinking about composition. It was going to allow him to program some of his favorite ideas about culture and man, for soon after he'd taken the job, he was writing, producing, and directing his own shows. Typical of Desnos, who as a boy had loved Nick Carter detective novels, his first success was a production of his *Fantomas,* a detective story in verse. And, typical of the man who scorned the distinction between elite and popular culture and confessed to a "mania for moralities," he created a show that dramatized historical and cultural subjects, often with music, to instruct and delight an audience of working men and women after their long, tiring day. But the program he loved best was *La clef des songes,* when listeners' dreams were read and interpreted according to a series of general symbols that had supposedly been passed on since antiquity but which he updated for the twentieth century: chariots becoming cars; birds, airplanes. In his own version of the Surrealist aim, he searched for correspondences between the dreams and the political events of a particular week. The work satisfied his need to be in touch with the common man; the same need that had extended the reach of his own poetry. But like all commonplace activities throughout Europe, it ended in the summer of 1939. Desnos was mobilized, leaving with some million others to wait out the long months of *la drôle de guerre,* returning with them to civilian life after the humiliating surrender and the traitorous establishment of the Vichy government under Petain, whom Desnos satirized under the name "Marechal Ducono." Soon he was working for *Aujourd'hui,* the new journal of a longtime friend, writing his precious columns of art and music commentary—he despised formal criticism, calling it the practice of "the illusory gifts of the intelligence on an autopsy of human works." Instead, he used his absolute trust in his own responses to a work: "I have good ears, I hear. I've heard Varèse's music, I'm therefore qualified to speak of the emotions experienced." The aim of his writing was always to encourage emotional responses to art, music, and poetry. A decade earlier, he had published a number of articles on the consoling power of the female voice. In 1940 he was telling his fellow citizens that despite everything, there would be singing in Paris that winter, as there had always been.

During the Occupation years, he worked on a number of projects: new poems, a moralizing anti-drug novel, and a collection of poems of the previous decade, *Fortunes,* published in 1942. In the afterword he noted "progress in the search for a poetic language, at once popular and precise," and an interest—if he were to have world enough and time—in studying mathematics and physics, with "the ambition of making 'Poetics' a chapter of Mathematics," because, he asks, "isn't poetry a science of numbers?" This book was followed, in 1943, by *État de veille,* whose title, which may be translated as "Awake" or "Waking State," has both the political connotation of being on the lookout for, aware, and the literary one of being in conscious control, not asleep or under the spell of psychic automatism. It contains many of his best poems from the 1936 experiment, as well as a number of "verses" or "couplets," ballads he wrote in the hope they'd be set to music and improvised upon. Some, like "Verses on rue Saint-Martin," make allusions to the Occupation, as do a number of other poems such as "Seasons," "Tomorrow," and "Time of the Dungeons," poems he referred to as "more classical in appearance," "part of a continuing experience whose evolution is impossible to predict and which I can't speak clearly of." Several more of these, such as "The Promontory," "Summer Dusk," and "Hello From the Valley," were to have been published in a retrospective volume of much of his work since the twenties, a volume which was to have included "Ars Poetica," his most powerful statement that poems are dragged up out of the muck of life, not made in universities and living rooms.

The last book published before his arrest, *Contrée (Country),* can be considered the finished product of that "evolution" he speaks of. It is made up of twenty-five poems written in alexandrines or syllabics, many of which are sonnets or resemble them, in that a carefully controlled movement of ideas through a series of stanzas leads to a concluding statement that has the feel of a couplet. Many of them, like "Cascade," contain allusions to classical mythology that, read between the lines, are a direct commentary on the Occupation, which Desnos had committed himself to working against from the moment of his return to Paris after the surrender. Using a series of pseudonyms, he published poems calculated to rouse, console, and offer hope—directly, not in the allusive fashion of poems published under his own name—poems such as "Song of Taboo," "The Legacy," and, especially, "The Watchman of the Pont-au-Change," in which the poet sees himself "awake in the heart of Paris" and "watching over the whole world that surrounds and crushes us." In this great *cri de coeur* the prophetic voice of Robert Desnos, first heard in "Ebony Life" twenty years earlier, then in "To the Headless" a decade later, calls out to all victims of fascist oppression to continue the struggle, assuring them of victory at last:

> *Let my voice come to you*
> *Warm, joyful, and determined. . . .*
> *On the threshold of the new day we wish you good morning*

The Gestapo came for him on the morning of February 22, 1944, looking for a list of names of Resistance workers they knew Desnos had. Loyal to the end, Robert had refused to escape, fearing Youki would be tortured in his place. A neighbor gave him a heavy shawl woven of Scottish wool which would serve him well in the cold, damp winter of Buchenwald.

After being interrogated, he was sent to Compiègne. It was almost a lark. He wrote. He was at the center of a group that met to discuss literature and astrology—Desnos told them he had considered reading palms professionally. But his luck changed, and he ended up at Buchenwald, where he sent his last hopeful letter to Youki. From there comes the story of Desnos moving through the ranks of a group of the doomed, awaiting the gas chamber, reading their palms, predicting happiness and long life . . .

With the Allies pushing toward Berlin, the camps were abandoned and the prisoners force-marched to the east. When order broke down and their guards fled, the prisoners, now free but weak—many of them, like Desnos, dying of typhus—staggered along the roads. Somehow, Desnos managed to reach Terezin, which the Allies now occupied. He was recognized by Josef Stuna, a Czech student who, along with Alena Tesarova, a nurse, spent his last days with him. They remember that Desnos smiled often and spoke of poetry and Paris. He died clutching a rose the nurse had given him.

Born at the beginning of a century whose horrors are still unfolding, Robert Desnos was one of millions of victims of a force that still threatens: the will of the modern state. At certain times and places, the official face of the state has smiled, and perhaps change is coming even in places where the face has been up till now implacable. But however benevolent any state may become, we will never return to the freedom of field, farm, and countryside; the magic of a little building in the corner of a square, dark side streets, beautiful moons rising over our cities. That world has been dead since 1945. What, then, of the message of Robert Desnos's greatest poems?—that life is good, that we can be happy if we are content to live fully through our senses, in unison with the seasons of earth and the **XXV**

seasons of our lives? That imagination is a power; that it can change our lives? In a time of terrible excess and cynical despair, these poems seem innocent. Yet even if they are, they may have the power to light up that tiny space inside each of us that still remembers the hope we felt as children, the sense of glory in the odors of the earth, joy in the blue sky.

Someday soon, I have no doubt, there will be a scholarly, definitive edition of the complete poems of Robert Desnos in English, perhaps in time for his centennial. It will be a huge task, not in the least because many of his poems will defy translation: the spoonerisms, the homonym poems, the ballads and Resistance poems written in slang. Examples of these could not be included in this selection. What I have selected are poems from every age and every stage of his work, poems I purposely chose to reflect as many different subjects, styles, moods, and attitudes as was possible in a volume of this length. Those who feel they know Desnos's work will no doubt argue for the exclusion of such and such a work or the inclusion of another. So be it.

The chief difficulty in translating Desnos lies in rendering the beauty of his dislocated syntax, says my colleague at the Community College of Philadelphia, Lucy Aghazarian, of the French Department. I owe her a debt of thanks for helping me wrestle my share of these poems into shape, as well as for helping me avoid the obvious mistakes. I am, of course, responsible for all that remain.

Otherwise, translating Desnos has presented the same basic danger any translation presents: loss of everything in the original, the sense of a living context for the words, their emotional overlays and resonances. I have tried to capture his voice in this language: meaning to reconstitute, where I could, in parallel form, searching for available equivalents, the emotional ground of any poem. Where the effort has been a success, the result has been a poem that satisfies in American English both my sense of audience and of Desnos himself.

—William Kulik
Philadelphia, 1990

[1] *For some of these facts and for some that will follow, I am indebted to Marie-Claire Dumas's excellent bio-critical study of Desnos, which forms the introduction to her analysis of his work,* Robert Desnos, ou l'exploration des limites *(Paris: Klincksiek, 1980).*

[2] *Man Ray recalled that Desnos could fall asleep in the middle of a sentence, wake up half an hour later and continue what he'd been saying.*

The time of the crusades is coming.
Through the closed window the birds insist on speaking
like fish in an aquarium.
In a shop window
a pretty woman is smiling.
Happiness, you're only sealing wax
And I vanish like a will-o'-the-wisp.
A great many keepers are chasing
a harmless butterfly escaped from the asylum.
In my hands it becomes a pair of lace pants
and your eagle-flesh
o my dream when I stroke you!
Tomorrow we'll bury for free
we'll no longer catch cold
we'll speak the language of flowers
we'll be enlightened by lights unknown to us now.
But today is today.
I feel my beginning is near
like the wheat in June.
Police, pass me your handcuffs.
The statues turn away without obeying.
I'll write insults on their pedestals and the name
of my worst enemy.
Down in the ocean
Underwater
the body of a beautiful woman
Drives the sharks away.
They climb to the surface, are mirrored in the open air,
and do not dare gnaw those breasts
those luscious breasts.

C'est les bottes des sept lieues cette phrase 'Je me vois'

DOOR TO THE SECOND INFINITY

The inkwell periscope lies in wait around the bend
my penholder goes back into its shell
The sheet of paper spreads its huge white wings
Before long its claws
will tear out my eyes
I won't see anything but my late body
my late body!
You had the opportunity to view it in full dress
the day of all ridicule
The women put their jewels in their mouths
like Demosthenes   .
But I'm the inventor of a telephone
made of crystal and
English tobacco
with a direct line
to fear!

C'est les bottes des sept lieues cette phrase 'Je me vois'

The temple entrance puts on eyeliner
Olympus and paradise and forests
Like the old electric bulbs
Now poetry is sucked from a pointed tit
from these homicidal luminous breasts
Thunderstorm is a make of car for
the invisible lovers of light
Gun barrels like so many heroes' mouths
cut out their tongues and throw them at insolent hearts
Love like fish swims in acid
The main generator the main generator
right the main generator what what
the nightingale! the one from Japan
Earth ocean and your breast tremble
and the armies like an avalanche
I'm telling you they'll have my head
o death
handsome mountain-climber in the armor of the white prince!

C'est les bottes des sept lieues cette phrase 'Je me vois'

ANNOUNCEMENT

On the deck of a ship a dressmaker is stitching
dressmaker cut me a big mercury peacock
this evening I'm taking my last communion
The last swallow makes an autumn
A face without meaning rises
From the pale gaslight
Glass statues flask simulacrum of love
Comes the famous lady
Postman of subtraction
with a letter for me
Dear Desnos my dear Desnos
I'll be seeing you
in a few days
You'll be notified
You'll put on your out-of-this-world dress suit
And everyone will be quite happy.

C'est les bottes des sept lieues cette phrase 'Je me vois'

WHAT DO YOU WANT ME TO SAY?

It's the pure truth
Like a mantle
My lovely lady put your hands
in the gas lamp
we'll see more clearly
You're lost if you can't scratch me
a little bit
to see
more clearly
A boat stops and makes its
will
Wheatfields cry loud and long for the frigate-bird's
hairstyle.
The mysterious concierge cautiously sinks
her key into your eye
after twenty years you're asked for your name
but the future doesn't need an i.d.
for your desires
Mine are simple
Let them keep me in booze my whole death long
And leave me in war.

C'est les bottes des sept lieues cette phrase 'Je me vois'

BUT I WAS NOT UNDERSTOOD

What corolla have you hidden your thumbs in?
Muzzle and handcuff love
You keep me from counting the days.
But the nights, there isn't one you don't speckle.

A tidal wave is washing the houses.
Right now they're blue.
Mountain ridges where memory is cut in two;
each side going limp
spattering my eyes with orange.

God's name is a well-polished copper plate
on the gate of heaven,

but wipe your hands before praying.

C'est les bottes des sept lieues cette phrase 'Je me vois'

If I like trains it's no doubt because they go faster
than funerals
last tango you're only a bugle-call at the end of
a corridor
I'm slowly threading locks between my fingers
The crime describes a parabola and falls back heavily
on its feet
You and that other you and that other one, you won't get away
The hanging rivers swing with the phases of
the moon
The prodigious tide begins at last
lovers come from everywhere
hummingbird ones
rose ones
Liberty a beautiful drowned woman of touching white aluminum
floats on the waves
Pretty soon she'll be taking off
and we won't recognize her anymore
Help!
I'm drowning!

C'est les bottes des sept lieues cette phrase 'Je me vois'

YOUR LOVERS
AND MISTRESSES

You don't write your initials with chalk
in the white forest of love.
A grim reaper erases the boards
of the calculators
gelatine city kind to spiders, my voice
makes you tremble.
Smoke plays a large part in my life.
And some ferocious tiger traced
the reflection of his yellow eyes on my chest.
An outer wall of tobacco and iris
That's the fort
of the tribunal of the
river where a hundred fish are fluttering.

C'est les bottes des sept lieues cette phrase 'Je me vois'

On your way!
Evening raises its white stick above the pedestrians.
Cowhorns in evenings of plenty you sow
terror on the boulevard.
On your way!
it's the scroll of the hour, bizarre, luminous.
Struggle to the death. The referee counts to 70.
The mathematician wakes up and says
"I was so hot!"
Supernatural children dress like you and me.
Midnight adds a strawberry pearl to Madeleine's necklace
then the doors of the station are slammed shut.
Madeleine, Madeleine, don't look at me that way
with peacocks flying out of your eyes.
The ashes of life are drying up my poem.
In the empty square invisible madness makes footprints
in the wet sand.
The second boxer wakes up and says
"I was so cold."
Noon the hour of love delicately tortures
our sick ears.
A very wise doctor sews the hands of the praying woman
assuring her she'll sleep.
an expert chef blends poisons on my
plate
assuring me I'll laugh.
I certainly will.
the pointed sun, hair is called romance in
the language I speak with Madeleine.
A dictionary gives the meaning of proper names:
Louis means roll of the dice,
André means reef,

10   Paul means etc. . . .
      But your name is dirty:
      On your way!

      C'est les bottes des sept lieues cette phrase 'Je me vois'

The disciples of light never invented anything but
not very heavy darkness.
The river rolls the body of a little woman and that means
the end is near.
The widow in a wedding gown gets into the wrong procession.
We'll all arrive late at the grave.
A ship of flesh is swallowed by the sand of a little beach.
The helmsman invites the passengers to be quiet.
The waves wait impatiently. Nearer, my God, to Thee!
The helmsman invites the waves to speak. They do.
Night seals its bottles with stars and makes a fortune
in the export trade.
Huge stores are built to sell nightingales.
But they can't satisfy the desires of
the Queen of Siberia who wants a white one.
An English commodore swears he'll never again be caught
picking sage at night between the feet of salt statues.
Apropos of this a little Cerebos salt-shaker gets up
with difficulty on its delicate legs. It pours
what's left of my life onto my plate.
Enough to salt the Pacific Ocean.
Put a lifebuoy on my grave.
Because you never know.

C'est les bottes des sept lieues cette phrase 'Je me vois'

O sorrows of love!
How dear and essential you are.
My eyes shut on imaginary tears,
hands forever reaching out to emptiness.
    Last night I dreamed of insane landscapes and adventures
as dangerous from the point of view of death as from
that of life, which are also the point of view of love.
    When I woke up you were there, sorrows of love, desert muses,
demanding muses.
    My laughter and my joy crystallize around you.
It's your makeup, your powder, your rouge,
your snakeskin bag, your silk stockings . . .
and it's also that little fold of skin between the ear and the nape,
where the neck begins, it's your silk slacks, your delicate blouse
and your fur coat, your round belly, it's my laughter and my joys
your feet and all your jewels.
    How really well-dressed and good-looking you are.

    O sorrows of love, demanding angels, there I go
picturing you as my love, confusing you
with her . . .
    Sorrows of love that I create and dress,
you get confused with my love about whom I know only
her clothing and her eyes, her voice, her face, her hands,
her hair, her teeth, her eyes. . . .

À la mystérieuse

I'VE DREAMED OF YOU
SO MUCH

I've dreamed of you so much you're losing your reality.
Is there still time to reach that living body and kiss
onto that mouth the birth of the voice so dear to me?

I've dreamed of you so much that my arms, accustomed
to being crossed on my breast while hugging your shadow,
would perhaps not bend to the shape of your body.

And, faced with the real appearance of what has haunted
and ruled me for days and years, I would probably
become a shadow.

O sentimental balances.

I've dreamed of you so much it's no longer right
for me to awaken. I sleep standing up, my body exposed
to all signs of life and love, and you
the only one who matters to me now, I'd be less able
to touch your face and your lips than the face and the lips
of the first woman who came along.

I've dreamed of you so much, walked so much, spoken
and lain with your phantom that perhaps nothing more is left me
than to be a phantom among phantoms and a hundred times more
    shadow
than the shadow that walks and will joyfully walk
on the sundial of your life.

À la mystérieuse

In the night there are of course the seven wonders
of the world and greatness tragedy and enchantment.
　　Forests collide with legendary creatures
hiding in thickets.
　　There is you.
　　In the night there's the walker's footsteps the murderer's
the town policeman's light from the streetlamp and the ragman's
lantern
　　There is you.
　　In the night trains go past and boats
and the fantasy of countries where it's daytime. The last breaths
of twilight and the first shivers of dawn.
　　There is you.
　　A piano tune, a shout.
　　A door slams. A clock.
　　And not only beings and things and physical sounds.
　　But also me chasing myself or endlessly going beyond me.
　　There is you the sacrifice, you that I'm waiting for.
　　Sometimes at the moment of sleep strange figures are born
and disappear.
　　When I shut my eyes phosphorescent blooms appear and fade
and come to life again like fireworks made of flesh.
　　I pass through strange lands with creatures for company.
　　No doubt you are there, my beautiful discreet spy.
　　And the palpable soul of the vast reaches.
　　And perfumes of the sky and the stars the song of a cock
from 2000 years ago and piercing screams in a flaming park
and kisses.
　　Sinister handshakes in a sickly light and axles grinding
on paralyzing roads.
　　No doubt there is you who I don't know, who on the contrary
I do know.
　　But who, here in my dreams, demand to be felt without ever
　　　　appearing.

You who remain out of reach in reality and in dream.

You who belong to me through my will to possess your illusion
but who bring your face near mine only if my eyes are closed
in dream as well as in reality.

You who in spite of an easy rhetoric where the waves die
on the beach
where crows fly into ruined factories, where the wood rots
cracking under a lead sun.

You who are at the depths of my dreams stirring up a mind
full of metamorphoses leaving me your glove
when I kiss your hand.

In the night there are stars and the shadowy motion of the sea,
of rivers, forests, towns, grass and the lungs
of millions and millions of beings.

In the night there are the seven wonders of the world.

In the night there are no guardian angels, but there is
sleep.

In the night there is you.

In the daylight too.

À la mystérieuse

Far from me and like the stars, the sea
and all the trappings of poetic myth,
Far from me but here all the same without your knowing,
Far from me and even more silent because I imagine you
endlessly.
Far from me, my lovely mirage and eternal dream,
you cannot know.
If you only knew.
Far from me and even farther yet from being unaware of me
and still unaware.
Far from me because you undoubtedly don't love me or,
what amounts to the same thing, that I doubt you do.
Far from me because you consciously ignore my passionate desires.
Far from me because you're cruel.
If you only knew.
Far from me, joyful as a flower dancing in the river
at the tip of its aquatic stem, sad as seven p.m.
in a mushroom bed.
Far from me yet silent as in my presence and still joyful
like a stork-shaped hour falling from on high.
Far from me at the moment when the stills are singing,
at the moment when the silent and loud sea
curls up on its white pillows.
If you only knew.
Far from me, o my ever-present torment, far from me
in the magnificent noise of oyster shells crushed
by a night owl passing a restaurant at first light.
If you only knew.
Far from me, willed, physical mirage.
Far from me there's an island that turns aside when ships pass.
Far from me a calm herd of cattle takes the wrong path
pulls up stubbornly at the edge of a steep cliff,
far from me, cruel woman.

Far from me, a shooting star falls into the poet's nightly bottle.

He corks it right away and from then on watches the star enclosed
in the glass, the constellations born on its walls,
far from me, you're so far from me.

If you only knew.

Far from me a house has just been built.

A bricklayer in white coveralls at the top of the scaffolding
sings a very sad little song and, suddenly, in the tray
full of mortar, the future of the house appears: lovers' kisses
and double suicides nakedness in the bedrooms strange beautiful
women
and their midnight dreams, voluptuous secrets caught in the act
by the parquet floors.

Far from me,

If you only knew.

If you only knew how I love you and, though you don't love me,
how happy I am, how strong and proud I am, with your image
in my mind,
to leave the universe.

How happy I am to die for it.

If you only knew how the world has yielded to me.

And you, beautiful unyielding woman, how you too
are my prisoner.

O you, far-from-me, who I yield to.

If you only knew.

À la mystérieuse

No, love is not dead in this heart these eyes and this mouth
that announced the start of its own funeral.
    Listen, I've had enough of the picturesque, the colorful
      and the charming.
    I love love, its tenderness and cruelty.
    My love has only one name, one form.
    Everything disappears. All mouths cling to that one.
    My love has just one name, one form.
    And if someday you remember
    O you, form and name of my love,
    One day on the ocean between America and Europe,
    At the hour when the last ray of light sparkles
on the undulating surface of the waves, or else a stormy night
beneath a tree in the countryside or in a speeding car,
    A spring morning on the boulevard Malesherbes,
    A rainy day,
    Just before going to bed at dawn,
    Tell yourself—I order your familiar spirit—that
I alone loved you more and it's a shame
you didn't know it.
    Tell yourself there's no need to regret: Ronsard
and Baudelaire before me sang the sorrows
of women old or dead who scorned the purest love.
    When you are dead
    You will still be lovely and desirable.
    I'll be dead already, completely enclosed in your immortal body,
in your astounding image forever there among the endless marvels
of life and eternity, but if I'm alive,
    The sound of your voice, your radiant looks,
    Your smell the smell of your hair and many other things
will live on inside me.
    In me and I'm not Ronsard or Baudelaire.
    I'm Robert Desnos who, because I knew

and loved you,
    Is as good as they are.
    I'm Robert Desnos who wants to be remembered
    On this vile earth for nothing but his love of you.

À la mystérieuse

THE WAY A HAND AT
THE MOMENT OF DEATH

The way a hand is raised at the moment of death or shipwreck
like the rays of the setting sun
your looks fly out in all directions.
There's no more time left, maybe no more time to see me,
But the falling leaf and the turning wheel tell you
nothing on earth lasts forever.
Except love,
and I need to convince myself of that.
Lifeboats painted shades of red,
Fleeting storms,
An old-fashioned waltz carried by time and the wind
through the wide-open spaces of the sky.
Landscapes.
The only embrace I need is the one
I long for,
And let the cock's crowing die.
The way a fist is clenched at the moment of death,
my heart is gripped by pain.
As long as I've known you I've never cried.
I love my love too much to cry
You'll cry on my grave.
Or I on yours.
It won't be too late.
I'll lie. I'll say you were my mistress,
Though there's really no point to it:
You and I will soon be dead.

À la mystérieuse

To slip into your shadow under cover of night.
To follow your footsteps, your shadow at the window.
That shadow at the window is you and no one else;
it's you.
Don't open that window behind whose curtains you're moving.
Shut your eyes.
I'd like to shut them with my lips.
But the window opens and the breeze, the breeze
which strangely balances flame and flag surrounds my escape
with its cloak.
The window opens: it's not you.
I knew it all along.

À la mystérieuse

THE VOICE OF ROBERT DESNOS

So like a flower and a current of air
the flow of water fleeting shadows
the smile glimpsed at midnight this excellent evening
so like every joy and every sadness
it's the midnight past lifting its naked body
    above belfries and poplars
I call to me those lost in the fields
old skeletons young oaks cut down
scraps of cloth rotting on the ground and linen
    drying in farm country
I call tornadoes and hurricanes
storms typhoons cyclones
tidal waves
earthquakes
I call the smoke of volcanoes and the smoke of cigarettes
the rings of smoke from expensive cigars
I call lovers and loved ones
I call the living and the dead
I call gravediggers I call assassins
I call hangmen pilots bricklayers architects
assassins
I call the flesh
I call the one I love
I call the one I love
I call the one I love
the jubilant midnight unfolds its satin wings
    and perches on my bed
the belfries and the poplars bend to my wish
the former collapse the latter bow down
those lost in the fields are found in finding me
the old skeletons are revived by my voice
the young oaks cut down are covered with foliage
the scraps of cloth rotting on the ground and in the earth
    snap to at the sound of my voice like a flag of rebellion
the linen drying in farm country clothes adorable women

whom I do not adore
who come to me
obeying my voice, adoring
tornadoes revolve in my mouth
hurricanes if it is possible redden my lips
storms roar at my feet
typhoons if it is possible ruffle me
I get drunken kisses from the cyclones
the tidal waves come to die at my feet
the earthquakes do not shake me but fade completely
    at my command
the smoke of volcanoes clothes me with its vapors
and the smoke of cigarettes perfumes me
and the rings of cigar smoke crown me
loves and love so long hunted find refuge in me
lovers listen to my voice
the living and the dead yield to me and salute me
    the former coldly the latter warmly
the gravediggers abandon the hardly-dug graves
    and declare that I alone may command their nightly work
the assassins greet me
the hangmen invoke the revolution
invoke my voice
invoke my name
the pilots are guided by my eyes
the bricklayers are dizzied listening to me
the architects leave for the desert
the assassins bless me
flesh trembles when I call

the one I love is not listening
the one I love does not hear
the one I love does not answer.

December 14, 1926

Les Ténèbres

IDÉE FIXE

I bring you a little bit of seaweed tangled with sea spray
    and this comb
But your braids are better tied than the clouds with the wind
    with the crimson sky and those with the quiverings of life
    and sobs that twisting sometimes between my hands die with
    the waves and the reefs along the shore in such numbers that
    for a long while we'll despair of perfumes and their flight
    at evening when this comb without moving points to the stars
    buried in their rapid silky flow crossed by my fingers
    forever searching their roots for the damp caress of a sea
    more dangerous than the one this seaweed was gathered from
    with the froth scattered by a storm
A dying star is like your lips
They turn blue like wine spilled on a tablecloth
An instant passes with the depth of a mine
The hard coal with muffled grumbling falls in flakes
    on the town
How cold it is in the dead-end street where I knew you
A forgotten number on a run-down house
Number 4 I think
I'll find you again before a few days are up near that pot
    of China asters
The mines snore hollowly
The roofs are covered with coal dust
This comb in your hair like the end of the world
The smoke the old bird and the jay
There roses and emeralds are finished
The precious stones and the flowers
The earth crumbles and goes star-shaped with the sound of an iron
    on mother-of-pearl
But your hair so well-braided is shaped like a hand

Les Ténèbres

I've lost my regret of evil with the passing years.

I've won the sympathy of fish.

Full of seaweed, the palace sheltering my dreams is a reef
as well as a territory of the stormy sky and not the washed-out
sky of gloomy religion

Even so I've lost the glory I despise.

I've lost everything but love, love of love,
love of seaweed, love of the queen of catastrophes.

A star whispers in my ear:

"Believe me, she's beautiful

The seaweed obeys her and the sea itself changes into
a crystal dress when she appears on the beach."

Beautiful crystal dress, you ring at the sound of my name.

Your vibrations, supernatural bell, live on
in her flesh

They make her breasts tremble.

The crystal dress knows my name

The crystal dress told me:

"The fury in you, the love inside

Child of the numberless stars

Master of the only wind and the only sand

Master of the carillons of fate and eternity

Master of everything finally except his lovely lady's love

Master of everything he's lost and slave to
what he holds on to.

You'll be the final guest at the round table of love.

The guests, the other thieves, have made off with
the silverware.

The wood splits, the snow melts.

Master of everything except his lady's love.

You who command the ridiculous gods of humanity
and do not use the power at your command.

You, master, master of everything except his lovely lady's love."

That's what the crystal dress said to me.

Les Ténèbres

SKY SONG

The flower of the Alps told the seashell: "You're shining"
The seashell told the sea: "You echo"
The sea told the boat: "You're shuddering"
The boat told the fire: "You're glowing brightly"
The fire told me: "I glow less brightly than her eyes"
The boat told me: "I shudder less than your heart does
   when she appears"
The sea told me: "I echo less than her name does in your love-making"
The seashell told me: "I shine less brightly than the phosphorus of
      desire
   in your hollow dream"
The flower of the Alps told me: "She's beautiful"
I said: "She's beautiful, so beautiful, she moves me."

Les Ténèbres

OF THE FLOWER OF LOVE AND THE WANDERING HORSES

In the forest lived a giant flower that risked killing
all the trees with her love
The trees all loved her
Toward midnight the oaks became reptiles and crept up
to her stem
The ashes and the poplars bent down toward her corolla
The ferns yellowed in her soil
And she was more radiant than the nightly love
of the sea and the moon
More pale than the huge extinct volcanoes of this star
More sad and more nostalgic than the sand dried and soaked
at the whim of the waves
I speak of the flower of the forest not of the tower
I speak of the flower of the forest not of my love
And if such a flower, more pale and nostalgic and adorable,
loved by the trees and the ferns, keeps my breath on her lips,
it's because we're of the same essence
I met her one day
I speak of the flower and not of the trees
In the forest shuddering when I passed
Welcome butterfly who died in her corolla
And you rotting fern my heart
And you my eyes nearly ferns nearly coal nearly flame
nearly wave
I speak in vain of the flower but of myself
The ferns have yellowed in the soil become like the moon
Like that exact instant in the agony of a bee lost
between a cornflower and a rose and a pearl
The sky is not so closed
A man appears, chrysanthemum in his buttonhole, who gives his
    name
and makes doors open
I speak of the impassive flower and not of the doors

to adventure and solitude
  One by one the trees died around the flower
  Which fed on their decay
  And that's why the plain became like the pulp of fruit
  Why towns sprang up
  A river at my feet winds and stops at my whim
a string of welcoming imagery
  Somewhere a heart stops beating and the flower straightens up
  The flower whose fragrance triumphs over time
  The flower that by itself revealed its existence to the plains
naked like the moon like the sea like the sterile atmosphere
of sad hearts
  A bright red lobster claw lies beside a pot
  The sun casts the shadow of the candle and the flame
  The flower straightens up with pride in a sky of invention
  Your nails my ladies are like its petals and red like them
  The forest murmuring low lays open
  A heart stopped like a dry spring
  There's no more time no more time to love you
who pass on your way
  The forest flower whose story I tell is a chrysanthemum
  The trees are dead the fields have turned green towns
have appeared
  The great wandering horses paw the ground in their
faraway stables
  Soon the great wandering horses leave
  The towns watch the herd pass through their streets
whose cobblestones ring with the clack of their hooves
and now and then glitter
  The fields are dug up by that cavalcade
  Tails dragging in the dust and nostrils smoking
they pass by the flower
  And for a long time their shadows remain
  But what has become of the wandering horses whose speckled hides
were a promise of misery
  Sometimes while digging in the earth someone comes across a
    strange fossil

It's one of their horseshoes
The flower that saw them still grows without blemish or weakness
The leaves grow out along its stem
The ferns blaze and bend toward the windows of houses
But what has become of the trees
The flower why does it flower
Volcanoes! O volcanoes!
The sky falls in
I think of the faraway of the deepest within me
Vanished times are like nails broken on closed doors
In the country when a peasant is going to die surrounded by
ripe fruit of the past season by the sound of frost cracking
on the windowpanes by boredom withered faded like the cornflowers
in the grass
The wandering horses appear
When a traveler loses his way in will-o'-the-wisps more broken
    than the lines
in old people's foreheads and lies down on the moving earth
The wandering horses appear
When a young girl lies naked at the foot of a birch and waits
The wandering horses appear
They appear in a gallop of broken bottles and grating cupboards
They disappear into a hollow
No saddles have worn down their spines and their glistening rumps
reflect the sky
They pass by spattering freshly plastered walls
And the frost cracking the ripe fruit the bare flowers the stagnant
    water
and the soft earth of marshes slowly changing shape
See the wandering horses pass

The wandering horses
The wandering horses
The wandering horses
The wandering horses

Les Ténèbres

With the tender and hard woods of these trees, with heart of oak
and birchbark, how many skies would you make, how many oceans,
      how many slippers
for the pretty feet of Isabelle the Vague?

With heart of oak and birchbark.

How many looks would you make with the sky, how many shadows
behind the wall, how many blouses for the body of Isabelle the Vague?

With heart of oak and birchbark, with the sky.

How many flames would you make with the oceans,
      how many reflections
bordering palaces, how many rainbows in the sky above
      Isabelle the Vague?

With heart of oak and birchbark, with the sky, with the oceans.

How many stars would you make with the slippers, paths
      in the night,
footprints in ashes, how many stairs would you climb to meet
      Isabelle the Vague?

With heart of oak and birchbark, with the sky, with the oceans,
with the slippers.

But Isabelle the Vague, you understand, is only a dream image seen
through the shiny leaves of the tree of life and death.

With heart of oak and birchbark.

Let her come to me to read in vain the strange lines of the fate
I hold in my clenched fist, which doesn't leave when I open my hand.

With heart of oak and birchbark, with the sky.

She can gaze at her face and hair in the depths of my soul
and kiss my mouth.

With heart of oak and birchbark, with the sky, with the oceans.

She can walk naked through the world, in the night, with me
    beside her,
terrifying the watchmen. She can walk on me, kill me, or die
    at my feet.

Because I love someone more moving than Isabelle the Vague.

With heart of oak and birchbark, with the sky, with the oceans,
with the slippers.

Les Ténèbres

A stalk stripped of its leaves in my hand is the world
The door is locked on the shadow and the shadow puts its eye
    to the keyhole
Here comes the shadow gliding into the bedroom
Here's the beautiful mistress a more carnal shadow than
    the great bird of white fur lost in blasphemy
        perched on the shoulder of the beautiful incomparable
    whore watching over her sleep imagines
The path is suddenly calm waiting for the storm
A green butterfly net swoops down on the candle
Who are you who take the flame for an insect
A strange battle between the gauze and the fire
I'd like to spend the night at your knees
At your knees
From time to time on your forehead shadowy and calm
    in spite of nocturnal apparitions I put a lock
    of dishevelled hair back in place
I'll watch over the slow sway of time and your breathing
This button I found on the ground
It's mother-of-pearl
And I'm looking for the buttonhole that lost it
I know your coat is missing a button
On the mountainside the edelweiss is withering.
The edelweiss flowering in my dream and in your hands
    when they open

An early good morning when drunkenness is shared when
    the adolescent river comes nonchalantly down
        the huge marble staircase with its retinue of white clouds
    and thistles
The most beautiful cloud was moonlight recently transformed
    and the tallest thistle was covered with diamonds
An early good morning to the flower of coal the kind-hearted virgin
    who'll put me to sleep tonight

An early good morning to the crystal eyes the lavender eyes
    the gypsum eyes eyes of dead calm eyes of sobbing
    eyes of storm
An early good morning greeting
The flame is in my heart and the sun in the glass
But never again alas will we say our
Good mornings to you all! crocodiles crystal eyes thistles
    virgin flower of coal kind-hearted virgin

Les Ténèbres

The green boughs dip when the dragonfly appears
    at the bend in the path
I approach a tombstone more transparent than snow
    white as milk as whitewash
    white as walls
The dragonfly wades in the pools of milk
The glass armor shakes quivers moves forward
Rainbows are tied à la Louis Quinze
What? already the ground hidden by our path
    raises its hand
Struggles with the glass armor
Knocks at doors
Floats in the air
Cries out
Moans weeps aaaaaaaah! wake you're dying
    in this noise blue rock
Huge chunks of sponge falling from the sky
    cover the graveyards
Wine flows with the sound of thunder
The milk the hidden ground the armor struggle on the grass
    which reddens and whitens by turns
The thunder and the lightning and the rainbow
Ah! wake you crack and sing!

The little girl goes off to school reciting her lesson.

Les Ténèbres

You can leave when you want to
The bed shuts unlacing itself with delight like
   a black velvet corset
And a shiny insect lands on the pillow
It gleams and returns to Darkness
The hammering waves roll in then are still
Samoa the beautiful sleeps all wrapped up
Hole in the ground what are you doing rolling those flags in the mud?
Under a lucky star under all the muck and mire
The wrecked ship is accentuated under the eyelid
I tell stories describing sleep
Collecting the flasks of night arranging them on a little shelf
The song of the wooden bird gets confused with the fragments
   of cork shaped like an expression
Don't go there not to die the joy is too great
One guest more at the round table in the clearing of emerald green
   and ringing helmets next to a pile of swords and dented armor
Nerve in the passionate lamp extinguished at the end of day
I sleep.

Les Ténèbres

A frightening stillness will mark that day
And the shadow of streetlights and fire-alarms
    will exhaust the light
All things, the quietest and the loudest, will be silent
The suckling brats will die
The tugboats the locomotives the wind will glide by
    in silence
We will hear the great voice which coming from far away
    will pass over the city
We will wait a long time for it
Then at the rich man's time of day
When the dust the stones the missing tears
    form the sun's robe on the huge deserted squares
We shall finally hear the voice.
It will growl at doors for a long while
It will pass over the town tearing up flags
    and breaking windowpanes.
We will hear it
What silence before it, but still greater the silence
    it will not disturb but will hold guilty
    will brand and denounce
Day of sorrows and joys
The day the day to come when the voice
    will pass over the city
A ghostly sea gull told me she loved me
    as much as I loved her
That this great terrible silence was my love
That the wind carrying the voice was the great revolt
    of the world
And that the voice would look kindly on me.

Les Ténèbres

What strange sound glided the length of the bannister down to where
    the transparent apple was dreaming?
The orchards were shut and far away the sphinx stretched out
    in the sand crackling with heat in the soft fabric of night.
Would that sound go on until the tenants woke up or slip away
    into the shadows of the morning mist? The sound persisted.
    The watchful sphinx had been hearing it for centuries and
    wanted to know it. So it wasn't surprising to see its supple
    silhouette in the shadows of the staircase. The beast scratched
    the waxed treads with his claws. The doorbells gleamed
    in the elevator shaft and the persistent sound sensing the arrival
    of the one shadow it had been waiting for among millions
    clung to its mane until suddenly the shadow faded.
This is the poem of the morning which begins while the restless woman
    in her cozy bed with hair undone pulled over her face and the sheets
    more wrinkled than her eyelids waits for the moment her door still
    closed on the floods of sky and night will open onto a landscape of
    resin and agate.
It's the poem of the day when the sphinx lies down in the restless
    woman's bed
    and in spite of the persistent sound swears faithful and eternal
    love.
It's the poem of the day which begins in the steaming odor of chocolate
    and the monotonous tap-tap of the floorwaxer amazed to see
        the claw marks
    of the night voyager on the stair treads.
It's the poem of the day which begins with matches sparking
    with the great horror of the pyramids surprised and saddened
    to no longer see their majestic companion lying
    at their feet.
But just what was that sound? Tell me while the poem of this day
    begins
    while the restless woman and her beloved sphinx dream
    of landscape in chaos.

38 It wasn't the sound of the clock or footsteps or a coffee-grinder.
What was that sound anyway? What was it?
Will the stairway plunge ever-deeper? Will it climb ever-higher?
Dream accept dreaming it's the poem of the new day.

Les Ténèbres

I fight furiously with animals and bottles
In a short time maybe ten hours have passed
   one after the other
The beautiful swimmer who this morning was afraid of the coral
   wakes up
The coral crowned with holly knocks at her door
Ah! coal again always coal
I'm begging you coal tutelary genius of dreams and my loneliness
   please let me speak again of the beautiful swimmer
   afraid of the coral
Stop tyrannizing this seductive subject of my dreams
The beautiful swimmer lay in a bed of lace and birds
Her clothes on a chair at the foot of the bed
   were lit by the last glimmers of the coal
Which, come from the depths of the sky the earth
   and the sea was proud of its coral beak and huge crepe wings.
All night long he'd followed funerals
   to suburban cemeteries
Had attended embassy balls left his fern-leaf mark
   on white satin dresses
Had risen terrible in front of ships
   and the ships had not returned
Now crouched in the chimney he was waiting for the foam to wake
   and the song of kettles
His ringing footstep had troubled the night silence
   in streets paved with resonant stones
Coal resonant coal master of dreams coal
Ah tell me where is she that beautiful swimmer that swimmer
   afraid of the coral?
But the swimmer herself went back to sleep
And I remain face to face with the fire where I'll stay
   all night long questioning the coal with its dark wings
     that persists in casting the shadow of its smoke
     and the terrible reflection of its embers on my monotonous path
Coal resonant coal merciless coal

Les Ténèbres

AT DAYBREAK

Will the schist light up the cork's sleepless night?
We'll be lost in midnight's corridor with the calm horror
    of a dying sob
Hurry all you lizards famous since antiquity climbing plants
    carnivores foxglove
Hurry creeping vines
Hiss of rebellion
Hurry giraffes
I'm inviting you to a feast so grand
The glasses will flash like northern lights
The women's nails will be strangled swans
Not very far from here the grass is wilting at the edge of a path

Les Ténèbres

The azure queen and the madman of the void go by in a cab
Heads of hair are leaning out each window
Calling: "See you soon!"
"See you soon!" say the jellyfish
"See you soon!" say the silks
Say the mother-of-pearl say the pearls say the diamonds
Soon a night of nights without moon or star
A night of all the seacoasts and all the forests
Night of all love and all eternity
A pane of glass shatters in a window being watched
A rag is flapping over the tragic countryside
You'll be alone
Among the bits of mother-of-pearl and the carbonized diamonds
The dead pearls
Alone among the silks which will be like empty dresses
    when you come near
In the wake of jellyfish fleeing when you look up
Maybe only the heads of hair won't run away
Will obey you
Will bend in your fingers like irrevocable condemnations
Short hair of the girls who loved me
Long hair of the women who loved me
And that I did not love
Stay a long while at the windows hair!
A night of all seacoast nights
A night of luster and funerals
A staircase unwinds beneath my feet and night and day reveal
    only shadows and disasters as my destiny
Only the huge marble column of doubt supports the sky
    above me
The empty bottles I smash into tiny dazzling shards
The smell of cork tossed back by the sea
Nets of fishing boats imagined by little girls

42   The bits of pearl being slowly ground to powder
      An evening of all the evenings of love and eternity
      The infinite profound sorrow desire poetry love revelation
          miracle revolution love the profound infinite envelops me
          in these babbling shadows
      Heads of hair the eternal infinities are shattered!
      It was it will be a night of nights without moon or pearl
      Without even broken bottles

      Les Ténèbres

LONG LONG AGO

Long long ago I went through the castle of leaves
Yellowing slowly in the moss
And far away barnacles clung desperately to rocks
   in the sea
Your memory better still your tender presence was there too
Transparent and mine
Nothing had changed but everything had aged at the same rate
   as my temples and my eyes
Don't you just love that platitude? let me go
   it's so rare for me this ironic satisfaction
Everything had aged except your presence
Long long ago I went through the surf
   on a lonely day
The waves were unreal even then
The hulk of the shipwreck you knew about—remember
   that night of storms and kisses?—was it a ship
   or a delicate woman's hat rolled by the wind
   in the spring rain?—was there too
After that it's happy horseshit and dancing in the hawthornes!
The aperitifs had changed the names and colors
Of the rainbows framing the mirrors.

Long long ago you loved me.

Les Ténèbres

NEVER ANYONE BUT YOU

NEVER ANYONE BUT YOU

Never anyone but you despite stars and loneliness
Despite the trees mutilated at nightfall
Never anyone but you will follow her path which is mine
The further you go the bigger your shadow gets
Never anyone but you will greet the ocean at dawn when I,
    worn out with wandering, coming through dark forests
    and nettle bushes, walk toward the foam
Never anyone but you will put her hand on my forehead
    over my eyes
Never anyone but you, and I renounce lying and unfaithfulness
You may cut the rope of this anchored ship
Never anyone but you
The eagle imprisoned in a cage slowly gnaws on the patina
    of the copper bars
What a deception
It's the Sunday marked by nightingales singing
    in the tender green woods the boredom of little girls
    staring at a cage a canary flutters around in while
    in the empty street the sun slowly moves its thin line
    along the hot sidewalk
We'll cross other lines
Never never anyone but you
And I alone alone alone like withered ivy in suburban gardens
    alone like glass
And you never anyone but you.

Les Ténèbres

The door is shut on the idol of lead.
Now there's nothing to make people notice
   that lonely house.
Perhaps only the water suspects something
The clear autumn mornings the rope around the neck plunge
   into the river
Never again will the forget-me-not little dog of Syracuse
   call the Persian-eyed farmer's wife with its ominous cry
From the time of Philippe le Bel across the crystal forests
   a loud cry comes and beats against the ivy-covered walls
The door is shut
Be quiet ah be quiet let the cold water sleep its deep sleep
Let the fish dive down toward the stars
The wind from the giant bed where murmurs rest
   the sinister wind of metamorphoses rises
Death to the teeth death to the white sail death to the everlasting
   summit
Let her sleep I say let her sleep or else
   I swear the earth will break open
That it will be all over between the moss and the coffin
I didn't say that
I didn't say a thing
What did I say?
Please, let her sleep
Leave the great oaks around her bed alone
Don't drive that shy, crumbling daisy
   out of her bedroom
Please, let her sleep.

Les Ténèbres

STARTLED

On the road back from the summits met by
    crows and chestnuts
Jealousy and the pale flatterer greeted
Finally the disaster disaster foretold
Why turn pale why shiver?
Jealousy and the animal kingdom greeted with fatigue
    confusion jealousy
A sail unfurling over bare heads
I've never spoken of my dream of straw
But where have the lonely theatrical trees all gone
I don't know where I'm going I have leaves in my hands
    leaves in my mouth
I don't know if my eyes closed last night on
    my precious shadows or on a river of gold and flame
Is it the day of encounters and pursuits
I have leaves in my hands leaves in my mouth.

Les Ténèbres

The huge white marble rose was alone on the empty square
   where shadows extended to infinity. And the marble rose,
   alone under the sun and the stars, was queen of solitude.
   And the odorless marble rose on her rigid stem at the top
   of a granite pedestal streamed with all the floods from
   the sky. The moon lingered pensive in her glacial heart
   and the goddesses of gardens the marble goddesses came
   to try their cold breasts on her petals.
The glass rose rang with all the sounds of the seacoast.
   No sob from a broken wave failed to make her tremble.
   Around her fragile stem and transparent heart rainbows
   revolved with stars. The rain glided in delicate circles
   down her leaves the wind sometimes set moaning in fear
   of streams and glowworms.
The coal rose was a black phoenix changed by face powder
   into a fiery rose. But flowing endlessly from dark corridors
   where miners picked her respectfully to carry her to
   daylight in her anthracite vein the coal rose kept watch
   at the doors to the desert.
The blotting-paper rose sometimes bled in the twilight when
   evening came to kneel at her feet. The blotting-paper rose
   guardian of all secrets and a bad counselor bled blood thicker
   than sea foam and which was not her own.
The cloud rose appeared over doomed cities at the time of volcanic
   eruptions at the time of fires at the time of riots and over Paris
   when the Commune mixed the iridescent veins of gas and the smell
   of powder she was beautiful on the 21st of January beautiful
   in the month of October in the cold wind of the steppes beautiful
   in 1905 at the time of miracles at the time of love.
The wooden rose presided at the gallows. It blossomed at the top
   of the guillotine then slept in the moss in the giant shadow
   of mushrooms.

48 The iron rose had been hammered for centuries by blacksmiths
        of lightning.
     Each of her leaves was large as an unknown sky. At the slightest
     shock she gave off a sound of thunder. But how kind she was
        the iron rose
     to despairing women in love.

The marble rose the glass rose the coal rose the blotting-paper rose
     the cloud rose the wooden rose the iron rose will go on flowering
     forever though today they lie on your rug leafless.

And who are you? you who crush beneath your bare feet the scattered
     remains of the marble rose the glass rose the coal rose the blotting-
     paper rose the cloud rose the wooden rose the iron rose.

Les Ténèbres

Women of high airs
Women facing strong winds
Is the night kind to you

Women facing strong winds
Wanderers met at dawn
Doesn't night tear you

Women of high airs
Plough women lost in the plains
Is the night a harvest for you

Women facing strong winds
Fishwomen with creviced hands
Does the night race by for you

Women awake at break of day
Women dragging to work on sore feet
Is the night echoless for you

Is the night kind?
Does the night tear you?
Do you harvest the night?
Does the night race by for you?

Women of high airs
Women facing strong winds
Women of night, dawn and day
Wanderers ploughwomen fishwomen
Do you like the high airs
Do you like the strong wind

Youki 1930 poésie

MERMAID

Once not upon a time
no one tried to break through the gates
of a beautiful castle in the heart of the desert
in a pool
there was a mermaid swimming

Once not upon a time
or rather yes, Once, Once upon a time
There is still in the heart of the desert
behind high walls
a mermaid swimming in a pool

Solitude silence lapless water
Nothing will come to disturb
the rhythmic swimming of the mermaid

It is she unchanging who calls
The movement of the hands on the dial
It is she who rules over the breathing
Over the lovers' and the sleepers' breathing

Over the breath of the one who dreams
Of the one who loves
Over the breath of the passionate lover

The storm rises in its money-changer uniform
Strides the horizon
Breaks against the hills
And in the splendor of the rainbow
Slips away as a fragrant river
Breaks against the colorful piles of prism

In the countryside kneeling
In a sweetly scented river
The mermaid is swimming
Immense in the sky at high tide
She passes above the fields
above the cities

The sheen of her scales is like lightning
It's her tail slowly sweeping
away the clouds

The landscape turns into sunlight
The mermaid goes back to her distant castle

All this can be seen
When the storm rumbles
When it flees beneath the rainbow

However there are other storms
Other landscapes of the heart
There are other mermaids.

Youki 1930 poésie

EVENING

In times past a heart beat in this breast
Once it beat only for her
The heart still beats but no one knows why anymore

It has sealed its lips forever
It doesn't say it will never say
the word love again

Perhaps the heart is still beating for her
It still certainly beats for her
But it beats in silence

It must be sad
The night of that one man
Who listens to his heartbeat

He listens to it beat as in the good old days
That time of delightful days
The days of illusion

But love has no right to be revealed
In the word of that relentless watchman
Determined to love and suffer

And if she also has a heart
One evening she will come stealthily
To close these eyes that fix her image in darkness

And put on the silence of this love
The immense and whistling silence of sleep
But then she will appear in a dream
And everything will start all over again

Youki 1930 poésie

The morning shatters like a stack of plates
In a thousand shards of porcelain and hours
And chimes
And waterfalls
On the zinc bars of this very poor bistro
Where starlight persists in the café night

She isn't poor
This one in her evening gown soiled with mud
But rich in the cold light of morning
In the stupor of her blood
And in the scent of her breath that no insomnia
    can sweeten
Rich in herself and all the mornings
Past present and future
Rich in herself and in the sleep that overcomes her
In the sleep strong as mahogany
In the sleep and the morning and herself
And in her whole life which can be counted
Only by mornings, bright dawns
waterfalls, sleeps
alive nights

She's rich, this one
Even if she holds out her hand
And sleeps come the fresh morning
In her filthy dress
on a barren bed

Youki 1930 poésie

To die without regret you have to be so weary
To die without regret for lost desires
To die without sorrow to die without pity
You must destroy the hands the eyes the faces too

Those women chosen among the races
born with a violent heart no love has bent
with hard limbs that nothing can bind
Know how to search for death among deep graves

But those who loved those who in their arms could keep
in the chill of sheets the lover or husband
to the point of defying the shadows

Will close both eyes during a night without fire
and throwing in their love like a final wager
Will know a rest as empty as the ruins

Youki 1930 poésie

The rose that blooms
on the banks of the Seine
Flowers after midnight
on the little lawns

On the little lawns
where sleep dances
where mermaids sing
Near Pontoise and Corbeil

Near Pontoise and Corbeil
with their lines in the water
Near Thommery and Creil
where old swans sing

where old swans sing
where the drowned run aground
If love is unworthy
and sells itself for money

And sells itself for money
where the rose flowers
You'll have to pay her well
If you love her for no reason

If she's loved for no reason
She flowers for no reason
She flowers this rose
By the Seine near Paris

In the Seine near Paris
Merry bodies float now
Gentle lovers and husbands
Down to the Havre harbor

56   Down to the Havre harbor
      where the steamships are being armed
      It is love that makes you grieve
      It is death that makes you afraid

      Youki 1930 poésie

Tom Thumb loses a slew of keys in the dark forest path
This is why so many doors are locked
Why your door is locked

Knock at the door at the window
A flickering light wanders from cellar to eaves
Your sleeping breath is heard

Are you a prisoner of your house?
Isn't the forest darkness calling out to you?
If you've lost the key to freedom
Then force the lock

Wake up
Don't breathe so peacefully
But above all
Above all turn out that light
that wanders while you sleep
that wanders from cellar to eave

Youki 1930 poésie

A DREAM IN A CELLAR

So many flasks were shattered in this cellar
that the odor of the wine drunk by the sand
Rose like an October fog above the old quays
And the saltpetered walls were lava yellow

While spinning her web the spider rocked
her fat belly stuffed with smoke
like a frigate at the hour when the tide
laps and spurts in the shadows like an abscess

Beautiful frigate that bears the name of a lover
A mermaid with brushed hair for your masthead
Would she have tossed you to the spider's fangs
That you so suddenly appear in her weave

Your sails filled by a delicate north wind
Blew you white into darkness
black as a restless sea and striped by foam swirling
on the rim of whirlpools

Beautiful frigate white as a shirt
Forgotten in a field by a laundress
On a starless night drying on a line
Beautiful frigate sail to the promised marvels.

Because no other sound is heard in this cell
but water crying in the heart of pipes
And footsteps of someone late coming
Dreaming again and again of the kindness of a warm bed.

Youki 1930 poésie

On the zinc bar of this little café the glass is shining
where night washes up at the border of day
where among scarves and shawls
Sobs rising in the drinker's throat
End in a burst of laughter

The glass is shining on the zinc bar of this little café
Because a drop still trembles at the bottom
A red drop like the stone
Not red like getting paid every last red cent no
But a beautiful jewel just the same

This is the hour when it would be good to wake up
to see the morning clearing
to listen to a footstep on the walk
The first window opening
And the morning friends calling to one another in the street

But still it is the hour when it's good not
   to sleep
even if you don't go to bed at all
when you're young and full of life
And when there is neither night nor day
To live and drink and sleep and sing

It feels good to be those
whom you still hear laughing and calling to each other
at dawn when you wake up
you people who sleep people with quiet hearts
whom one hears laughing by day when it's good to sleep

Youki 1930 poésie

THIS BEAUTY HERE

when age will have withered these eyes and this mouth
when too many memories will weigh down this heart
when only mocking ghosts will remain to rock
in this body's bed this body today beautiful

when vile dust covering things
shrouds abolished desires
when love more withered than a rose in a book
will be only a name under faded portraits

when it will be too late not to be cruel anymore
when the echo of kisses and the echo of vows
Will diminish like a footstep in the dark night alley
or the whistle of a train rising to the black heavens

when fingers hardened by passions
And weary of wiping too many sour tears
On sagging breasts and a creased belly
Will know again their debasement

when no makeup can lie to this face
As it leans toward the mirror once too kind
To relieve its thirst at a mirage
Of past dreams relived in the present

The beauty that is there will still be beautiful
By virtue of a fire always reflected
at the windowpanes of a castle whose echoing rooms
will be haunted by those who had been her lovers

The beauty here like a fountain
Whose stream always flowing pure on the cracked marble
Carrying ineffable mermaids
Will never stop trying to retain its splendor

Nothing will vanish from the reflected skies
Despite wrinkled skin and sagging loins
She'll still be envied there at the party
Forever young, this beauty

Once so many hearts beat expectantly for her
that a flame is enclosed in this body for no reason
that though unworthy of these fires she remains radiant
As the coals surviving a blaze

Youki 1930 poésie

My mermaid is blue like the veins where she swims
Right now she's sleeping on mother-of-pearl
And on the ocean I create for her
She can visit the magic caves of unlikely islands
Where some very stupid birds
Converse with endless crocodiles
And the very stupid birds fly above the blue mermaid
The crocodiles return to their drinking
The island cannot believe this
It does not return from where it is
Where my mermaid and I have forgotten it
My mermaid has very beautiful stars in her sky
Blond stars with black eyes
Red stars with shiny teeth
And brown stars with beautiful breasts
Every night three by three
alternating the color of their hair
Those stars visit my mermaid
This makes for a lot of back and forth in the sky
But the sky of my mermaid is no ordinary sky
My mermaid has seven boats on her ocean
Monday Tuesday Wednesday Thursday Friday
Saturday and Sunday
Some with steam engines others with sails
Some fast others slow
But all of them beautiful all of them charming
with sailors who know their work well

My mermaid has soaps of all shapes and colors
For washing her delicate skin
My mermaid has many soaps
One for the hands
The other for the feet

One for yesterday
One for tomorrow
One for each eye
And this one for her scaly tail
And this other one for her hair
And one more for her belly
And one more for her loins

My mermaid sings only for me
Although I tell my friends to listen
Nobody has ever heard her
Except one, only one
But even though he seems sincere
I don't trust him as he might be lying

Les nuits blanches

Today I'd like to write beautiful verses
Like those I read in school
Sometimes they turned my dreams upside down
It's also possible I'm a little nuts

But counting all those words connecting those syllables
Seems to me like the tedious work of an ant
I'd lose my Latin my Chinese my Arabic in it
And even sleep, my obliging friend

So I'll write as I speak and never mind
If some grammarian sprung from the half-light
Wanted to condemn me with anger and spite
I've got another science I can confuse him with

Les nuits blanches

THE SECOND SONG OF THE
MARIGOLD (The Flower of Worry)

Having said having done
What pleases me
I go right I go left
And I love the marigold

I go right I go left
I drink some wine I drink some water
Singing out of tune but singing loud
And I love the marigold

Singing out of tune but singing loud
If the devil were here
I would invite him
If he loves the marigold

I would invite him
As I invite all good comrades
To share my glass and song
And empty our glasses for the marigold

Les nuits blanches

THE RIVER
WITH WATER LILIES

The river with water lilies
Under the sweet shade of the tall poplars
flows between two bridges
where the cries of the boatmen ring louder

The frog in a dress with a train
Whose name is Pulcherie
meets Nepomucene there
The minnow lover she chose

Her croak of love wears out
before the longing silence of the fish
And the river water makes them tipsy
When the drinkers pour their glasses from the bridge

The fisherman with his line at an angle
Hasn't moved for thirty years
They say he died of oblivion on the job
And no one came to wake him up

The red bobber on his line
Is a little discolored
It's an old carrot that the moon
at midnight like a calf seems to graze on

The stars are enormous
The night in the sky over the town
And the songs of the drinkers
Seem unable to cross the ramparts

This town is not at all reassuring
It is said that from the spring

a figure at times comes out at dusk
Like a nude young girl from a mirror

It might very well be Ophelia
It might very well be Pulcherie
It might be Nepomucene
Minnow frog or the beautiful
Ophucene Nepomelie
Pulcherfrog or frogminnow
at the bank of the river with water lilies
that flows between two bridges

Les nuits blanches

when death sets its scales of justice on my breast
I hope, days of love, that you'll triumph
Over the days when my heart, beating in silence,
gives rise only to your echo to make me despair

I hope that my mouth surrendering to such kisses
Will never have risked them in vain
that the nights when love tore my shirt
also tore themselves apart to make us eternal

But the sad days when the swing of the bells
From the dungeon of my heart rings at my wrist
Like a pitiful coin and in the depths of some pocket
Rusts and clinks as a nagging regret

I disembark in a port without lighthouse or keeper
Where I discover at the end of a windy boulevard
My endless desires burning in effigy
Without sparks without heat almost without flame

And then I enter the unclaimed castles
where mirrors of forgetting seem to reflect
from hallway to hallway and if my mouth
wants to drink, it is at the magic waters of the Lethe

In tall parlors my days of happiness
Line up to dream of old times
And suddenly breaking from the dark chambers
Bells by the thousands ring themselves

And at the same time bronze striking bronze
Surrounds the dreaming woman with strong bars
Like the ones that Louis XI wished for La Ballue
or Bostock for his lions Lili for her birds

Impregnable cage with echoing walls
I find its solution in my torment and the heavens
drone less than this kingdom without dawn
This forest of sounds and this clamoring desert

And defying death, its scythe and its scales
I am very sure, days of love, that you'll triumph
over the days when my heart trembles in silence
my very heart that alone drives me to despair

Les nuits blanches

HELLO, GOOD-BYE

It is night be the flame
And the blush that colors the clouds
Hello sir Good-bye madam
You don't look your age

Who cares if your kisses
Make the astral twins bleed
Who cares if your face is painted
if the frost shines on the boughs

Of granite or marble
Your age will show
And the shadow of the tall trees
will stroll over your tombstones.

Les nuits blanches

MY LOVE SPEAK TO ME

When you love me, let me surrender
To your embraces
To soothe my torments my fears
    My love speak to me
We must fill the hostile nights
With passionate cries
We must charm the quiet nights
    My love speak to me

In the night doomed to evil spells
Ghosts spread fear
And you if you are not one of the dead
    My love speak to me

If you love me say it
You must prove your passion
You must prove your frenzy
    My love speak to me

Even if you tell me lies
if you fake your passion
So the dream can go on
    My love speak to me

Les nuits blanches

How strange it is to wake up sometimes in the middle of the night
In the midst of sleep someone knocked at the door
And in the extraordinary city of midnight, of half-waking and half-
　　memory
carriage doors ring out heavily from street to street

Who is this late visitor with an unknown face
what is he looking for what is he trying to find out
Someone begging for bread and board
Is it a thief a bird
A reflection of ourselves in the mirror
Returning from a transparent abyss
That tries to come back inside of us

He then notices that we've changed
that the key no longer fits the lock
Of our mysterious bodies anymore
Even if he left only a few seconds ago
at that anxious moment when you turn off the light

What becomes of him then
Where does he wander? is he in pain?
Is this the origin of ghosts?
the origin of dreams?
the birth of regrets?

Never knock at my door again visitor
There is no room in my hearth or in my heart
For the old images of myself
It may be that you recognize me
Me, I will never know if you recognize yourself

Les nuits blanches

I

You are neither beautiful nor rich,
Your love is a burden,
For the pain it brings to me
Your love is my fetish.

Let the bread harden
In the bottom of the sideboard
Too sincere indeed
You lose all when you cheat

You suffer without saying it
You cry in your laughter
You are really my lover

I am Lou the redhead
I am Lou the shark lady
I love you desperately

II

For the pain it brings me
Your love is a fetish to me
Let the buns harden
In the pit of my gut

In the café night
The hazy dear
Escapes in the fallow sky
To the lights of auto-da-fé

When you come nightly
To prowl like a crazy man
Near Lou the naughty

74   If you read the future
Tell me when the love
Thornier than an eglantine will die?

III
If death brushed me
with its amber comb
The sky would fall
July would be December

if death called me
It would become mute
The walls of its palace
Would fall on its head

I don't want to die
I'm drunk on my blood
let the others rot
let us survive them

And we will be able to sing of
Lou the gentle shark lady
Her heart and her beauty
Love and the wild eglantine

The rose in the eagle's beak
Exuding her perfumes
and the taste of rye
and our thirsts and hungers

And may our burning thirsts
our hungers and desires
beautiful lover dear lover
not be slaked

IV

You call me so insistently in a dream and so want to see me
that your dream reaches through the distance
And you appear at the fall of evening

I admire your love and cherish your constancy
It's not for seven years, like a scrap of mirror,
But for eternity that an imprudent glance
marked your fate with the seal of my power

I know what I can ask of your heart
It belongs to me and the fire that lights me
As much as it consumes you never dies

But I'm your victim as much as your conqueror
And like iron our love won its strength
From the blows of a heavy hammer on a stone anvil.

Les nuits blanches

O YOUTH

O youth, the wedding is over
The guests are leaving the banquet tables
The napkins are stained with wine and the waxed floor
Is scuffed white by the steps of the dancers and the dreams

A wave carried roses to the shore
some unhappy lover threw from the pier
Into the sea mourning relics and bouquets
And the kings have eaten the cake and its hidden charm

Flaming noon foretells twilight
The cemetery is crowded with friends jostling each other
may their sleep be calm and their deaths not too hard

But as long as there's wine in the bottles
let my glass be filled and my ears plugged
I will listen to the sea rise in my heart

Les nuits blanches

1

You've been singing for so long
Aren't you thirsty? Aren't you hungry?
I'm thirsty! But the spring is slow
I'm hungry! Will you love me tomorrow?

2

You didn't have those eyes my dear
All that April that was ours
I read a foreign phrase there
I see there the memory of others

3

My jealousy is like the snow
It's monotonous and still
It covers, it protects
All the glory of spring

Bagatelles

As beautiful as you are
With your lake and fire eyes
with your wolf-trap eyes
with your eyes, color of night and day, dawn and marjoram

As beautiful as you are
with your sharpened teeth and biting hard to the blood
with your deep sea teeth flashing

As beautiful as you are
with kisses always ready on your lips
with your lips of silence, turmoil, sweetness, and cruelty
with your lips too clear and at times too rushed

As beautiful as you are
with your wounded breasts and short-lived perfection
with your consoling breasts
with your breasts cupped in the palms like fruit

As beautiful as you are
with your hair and your belly
with your firm round belly
with your thicket of hair smelling strongly of you

As beautiful as you are
with your loins with your cold ass
with your wingbones easy to scratch
with your neck that would so easily be had

As beautiful as you are
with your delicious and sufficient sex
with your splendid sex
with your sex fanciful like you and bloody like your heart

Beautiful as you may be
I will not love you
Beautiful as you are

I am rebelling at last against such servitude.
I loved the most beautiful one and when she passed away
I loved an even more beautiful one who could have been her sister
I am breaking my chains
I fix my eyes to the light of this morning
at dawn at the hour of sleep
when old wounds open again
when absence and solitude howl

And that's when morning seems soft to me
familiar morning calm morning in spite of rain and lashing winds
morning for a good bath and a fresh heart

My new heart is harder than steel
and less cruel than your tender heart
I will not love I don't want to love anymore

Vultures dazed by blizzards and the simoon wind
slap like big tattered flags
scatter yourselves in the storms
birds of carrion birds birds of love

And who cares if I love again
It would only be a question of loving the same woman
and even if I loved her again
there'd be no question about it

Hardened by that love burning like a torture device
protected by it
there's no question of you, the others
deserts will keep us apart
and the stars as well

I know where some of them come from
and to what depths others go

I know what answer must be given
to the splendid words you utter
and those she utters
between midnight and three in the morning

Her heart was purer than the primeval forests
more entangled darker more terrible
than a universe of collapsed tunnels
of nocturnal abysses and walled prisons
As mysterious as yours are
I will from now on walk
as through a well-tended park

I disembark in a town sad like life
and monotonous like life
you can hear the sound of a hammer on nails
the engines hum you to sleep
the houses being built will only fall long after my death
and art is expressed there even in the funeral vaults.

For a kiss I will go into slavery again
but consciously
To live this way or the other
all monotonous, the same

Life is beautiful however
the least sincere kisses
still leave the delicious taste of delirium and love
between the teeth

We will die in our eighties
if that is our fate
and the sound of hammers on iron nails
will be the same the morning after

But above all I don't want to love anymore
My memories that are made only of present and future
are passionate enough to occupy all my life.

Like a trapped animal I escape
The gun of the poacher and his snare
will not get hold of me
As beautiful as you are
and how beautiful she was my poacher love

Find yourself a path other than mine

Sadly I greet you, morning
sadly with a heart full and empty
but with a measure of health and courage

Beautiful as you are
Go away from me.

Bagatelles

The room is closed and empty, very empty
Only the sun, at certain hours, shifts its line
   on the tangled blankets and creased pillow;
A dress, on a chair, moves with the breathing
   of a mysterious wind
And a hair quivers on the folded sheet,
And the clock that is ticking still and will soon stop,
   sings in the desert.
Evening hummingbird, morning hummingbird
My beautiful hummingbird enters the room,
Flaps its wings,
Bursts into vivid colors on the pillow.
The rainbow fades in the sky around the flower-beds of stars.
My beautiful hummingbird, hummingbird of evening and morning.
Fly.
Bump your delicate head into your double in the mirror's
   flaking patina.
Bleed.
Die.
My beautiful hummingbird of evening and morning.
Swollen stomach,
Bleeding beak,
Open wings,
Stiffened legs,
Die
So that in the empty room the sun can shift its line
   around your corpse
Where the window is reflected in the blood that thickens your down.
For an identical song, for the same flight,
Wearing the same colors,
Evening hummingbird, morning hummingbird
You will be born again.
And in the empty room, the clock will tick again

Hummingbird, hummingbird,
Evening hummingbird, morning hummingbird.

The bird that flies toward the coast
isn't near the shore where, puckering their lips
The earth's sky and the sea's sky
share a foam kiss.

It isn't flight's fault that the bird is lost at sea,
nor the fault of the sailor who gazes vacantly from the ship,
maidenhead, figure in a dream
the very image of the one he loves.

This one who passes far from all continents,
Far from the grassy continents where wild bulls run,
Far from the wet continents where the sea cow and hippopotamus
Paddle handsomely in the mud that gleams, dries out, and cracks apart,

Far from the continents of city and love,
Far from the continents of everlasting jealousy,
Far from the continents of steppe, snow, and sand
Far from the continents of sun

This one who goes where I want
To the country of mermaids and typhoons,
to the country of rumbling thunder
Near the continent of arid sky,
In the archipelago of eternal clouds.

Roll, roll, clouds, while the bird flies
Not far from there,
A bride-to-be receives for her celebration
The postcard of an eternal vow

The dove holds the sealed letter in its beak,
"I swear undying love."

Roll, roll, clouds, archipelago of clouds,
Ocean, dry ocean.

The fountains cry far from the birds
Far from the whisper of wind in the plane trees.
The fish that holds the mermaid full in its mouth
Spits water on the streetlamps' glow and the tarmac's glimmer

And this whole story comes to an end,
Far from the eye, the heart,
Near an eternal vow.
In Paris, on the place de la Concorde
The most beautiful and touching woman passes
Alone, on foot, sad.

And, far from her, beneath the sea
a bird flies
And the woman never sees the flight of this bird ever,
    the shadow of the bird's flight never crosses over
The path followed by the woman.
Never? Is this certain?
O, encounters—
O, crying fountains in the heart of cities
O, hearts crying for the world

Long live life!

The terrible bird, menacing,
Is on a branch of a dreadful tree
And death is hidden in a knife.
The laughter of the furious ones
Opens your mouth in vain.
I know you are condemned,
I refuse to save you

The tree is on fire
And death is written in capital letters,

Hanging by your hair,
Tied to your nape by underground flowers,
Mixed with your glances.

Your brow is an insult,
A stone in an abyss,
My tongue in my mouth.

I know there is no longer time.

Bagatelles

By loving so much, I lost myself in the sea. And what a sea!
A storm of laughter and tears.
If you climb aboard a ship, be careful to look at the figurehead that will
gaze at you with an eye eaten away by the wave and saltwater.

But what am I saying? The spectacles of love don't interest me very
much. All I want to be now is a sail blown by the pleasure
of the monsoons toward unknown continents where I will find
only one person. The one you
already have a perfect name for.

I undress, as an explorer lost on an island should, and I stay
immobile as a figurehead.

Hail to you, wind from afar, and you, desert, and you, forgetfulness.

I'll be forgotten. Someday no one will know my name, but I will
know hers.

One evening, naked in glory and rich, I will come back,
I will knock on her door,
completely nude, but no one will answer, even when,
having opened the door, I appear in her sight.

I have grasped, at least, the meaning of perpetuity. Not the
ridiculous one of cemetery plots.

I wish in vain for imaginary guillotines but can only offer the
bloodthirsty crowds my desire for suicide.

Revolution! You'll only shine after my death on the immense white
marble block that will cover my immense corpse.

France is a wasps' nest, Europe a rotted field, and the world a
peninsula of my consciousness.

But fortunately I still have the stars left and the consciousness of my
moral greatness opposed to the thousand obstacles the world
sets against my love.

Bagatelles

What are you doing in my glass little giraffe?
Giraffe of wine
Giraffe of breeze
Giraffe that tastes of milk and green leaves
What desert are you lost in?
Yes, it's the desert I drink in my glass
an arid desert more dead than a pile of bones
a lifeless desert, airless, without stars
the real desert of the end of the world
How could you get lost in this place far from any abyss
       and all borders?
Giraffe giraffe little giraffe of wine
But what stroke of luck led you under my pen?
Because I will make of this desert
of this desert drunk in my glass
a fiery oasis
a countryside full of the whisper of springs and
       and trees
a place of lawns and flowers
of juicy quartered fruits bleeding a perfumed blood
I'll fertilize this desert
with all the flowers of my immense love for life.

Mines de rien

INTERSECTION

In this intersection there's an air of memories,
    encounters, of strange, absurd, and very important things
The orange, the green flowering windows of the pharmacy
The enamel writings that can be read on the café glass
The song of the passerby is the same as anywhere else
The streetlight the same
The houses like so many others
Same pavements
Same sidewalks
Same sky
And still many people stop at this place
Many seem to detect there the scent of their own bodies
And the perfume of former loves
Irremediably lost in the agony of forgetting.

Mines de rien

LYING DOWN

On my right, the sky, on my left, the sea.
And in front of me, grass and flowers.
A cloud moves along vertically,
Parallel to the plumb-line horizon,
Parallel to a man on horseback.
The horse runs to its doom
While the cloud climbs endlessly.
How simple and strange everything is.
Lying on my left side,
I lose interest in the landscape
And think only of very vague things,
Vague and very pleasant,
Like the weary look that is turned,
This beautiful summer afternoon,
To the left, to the right,
Here and there,
In a frenzy of the useless.

Bagatelles

Men with foul tempers
Men of my two hands
Men of the early morning

The machine rolls at Deibler's command
And gear after gear in the odor of percolators
    that oozes out from under bar doors and the odor
    of hot croissants
The man who feels his socks stiffened by last night's sweat
and puts them on again
And his shirt stiffened by last night's sweat
And puts it on again
Who tells himself in the morning he'll wash up at night
And at night that he'll wash up in the morning
Because he's too tired . . .
And the one whose eyelids are glued together when he wakes up
And the one who wishes he had typhoid fever
So he could finally rest in his soft white bed . . .
And the emigrant who dines on nothing
While under his nose tasty leftovers from the first-class tables
Are thrown into the sea
And the one who sleeps in the subway and is chased by the station-
    master
    to the next station . . .

Men with foul tempers
Men of my two hands
Men of the early morning

Les sans cou

DON JUAN'S CITY

Blind men, cripples, idiots
Hunchbacks, cops and drunks
Shuffling along.

Enough steam to move a hundred ships.
The seven o'clock sirens cried out: "Time to get drunk."

Don Juan stopped at a place
Where I know there's a drinking-fountain
A fire-alarm and a wheelbarrow chained to a bench.

He stayed there until midnight,
Without getting bored,
Alone in the night.

At midnight, a woman in mourning
But naked under the huge veil on her hat
Appeared from a side street.

She was carrying a bottle of wine and a glass,
She was carrying a dead bird
She gave him the dead bird and a glass of wine.

A carriage door opened suddenly
A pretty girl with beautiful legs jumped out
And gave him her doll and a necklace of ebonies.

At a lighted window,
A woman was getting undressed
Throwing the hero her clothing piece by piece.

The flower-lady on the corner
Brought him all her roses
And a hag selling papers all her papers.

A very beautiful very repulsive woman
Showed him her watch
And told him it didn't work anymore.

A woman wearing wooden shoes, a peddler,
Came, holding up her apron.
In it, a fish like no other in the world.

She threw it in the gutter,
And the fish flopped around
Till it died.

The woman who won at baccarat,
The woman who just gave all her diamonds
   to her lover,
Came, too, through the streets and out of doors.

He brought some of them down from the sky
Like exhausted larks
He brought others up through the airholes in caves.

Some could have ruled empires
Others had filthy bodies and filthy minds.
Still others carried dread diseases.

But Don Juan smelled an icy, refreshing wind
In the breath of the next morning,
Smelling of low tide and oysters

Which blew in his leaves and his branches,
And his roots sucked hungrily at the sweets
Of earth, however poor it was.

His bark was tougher than armor-plate,
Beating stronger than an athlete's heart,
And he wasn't cramped in his iron corset.

94   He helped the lamplighter,
        The city sprinklers,
        The garbage collectors and the postmen on their daily rounds.

        For a handsome tree, he was a handsome tree.
        They cut him down the following day,
        They burned him and yet,

        His bitter sap was so potent
        And so many lovely women
        Had walked under his leaves

        That something of him remained
        In the fireplace when his ashes cooled,
        In the very hole where he had been.

        To tell the truth, not much is left of him,
        A hole in the sidewalk,
        A hole, nothing but an empty hole, a tiny hole.

        Les sans cou

There's a precise moment in time
When a man reaches the exact middle of his life.
A fraction of a second
A fleeting bit of time, quicker than a glance
Quicker than a fit of passion,
Quicker than light.
And a man is aware of this moment.

Long avenues with overhanging trees stretch out
Toward a tower where a lady sleeps
Whose beauty withstands kisses and seasons
Like a star the wind, like a rock the waves.

A quivering boat sinks bawling.
A flag waves at the top of a tree.
A well-dressed woman with stockings fallen to her ankles
Appears on a street corner
Flushed, trembling,
Protecting with her hand an old-fashioned lamp which is smoking.

And in addition a drunken stevedore sings in the corner of a bridge
And in addition a mistress bites the lips of her lover
And in addition a rose petal falls on an empty bed
And in addition three clocks toll the same hour
At several-minute intervals
And in addition a man passing in the street comes back
Because someone has called his name
But it is not he this woman is calling.
And in addition a public official in full dress
Cramped by his shirttail wedged
    between his pants and his underwear
Dedicates an orphanage
And in addition a wonderful tomato falls from a truck speeding

Through the empty streets and rolls into the gutter
To be swept away later
And in addition a fire breaks out on the seventh floor of a building
And burns in the heart of the silent and indifferent city
And in addition a man hears a long-forgotten song
That he'll forget again
And in addition many other things
Many other things a man sees at the precise moment of the middle of
    his life
Many other things happen for a long time
  in the briefest of brief instants on earth.
He ponders the mystery of that second, that fraction of a second,
But he says, "Let's get rid of dark thoughts"
And he gets rid of them.
And what could he say?
And what better could he do?

Les sans cou

The secret squats in the tall grass to rest
after an exhausting trip through deserted country.
Pursued, hunted, spied on, denounced, sold out.
Beyond all laws, all reach.
At the same moment cards are thrown down
And one man says to another:
"See you tomorrow"
Tomorrow he'll be dead or long gone from there.
At the moment when white curtains tremble on the deep night,
When the bed turned upside down on its posts gaping toward
    its missing innkeeper
Waits for some giant from beyond the horizon,
The secret squats, sleeping.
Don't make any noise, let the secret rest
In a corner of this page.

Fear it will wake up
More terrified than a bird colliding with furniture
and walls.
Fear it may be living with you,
Fear it may leave with all your windows broken,
Fear it may be hiding in a dark corner
Fear waking the sleeping secret.

Les sans cou

The last drop of wine flares up at the bottom of the glass
   where a castle has just appeared.
Gnarled trees at the edge of the road lean down toward the traveler.
He comes from the town nearby,
He comes from the distant city,
He simply passes by the foot of steeples.
He sees a red star moving in a window
Which comes down and walks wavering
On the white road into the black country.
It steers toward the traveler who watches it approach.
For an instant it shines in his eyes,
It settles on his forehead.
Stunned by the cold gleam which lights him up,
He wipes his forehead.
A drop of wine beads on his finger.
Now the man moves off and grows tiny
   in the night.
He has passed near the spring where you come in the morning to pick
   watercress.
He has passed near the abandoned house.
He is the man with the drop of wine on his forehead.
At this moment he is dancing in a huge room,
A brilliantly lit room
Its waxed parquet floor glistening
Deep as a mirror.
He is alone with his partner
In that huge room, and he dances
To the music of an orchestra of ground glass.
The creatures of night gaze
At this one couple dancing
And the most beautiful of the creatures of night
Mechanically wipes a drop of wine from his forehead,
Puts it back into a glass,

And the sleeper awakes,
Sees the drop shining like a hundred thousand rubies in the glass
Which was empty when he fell asleep.
Gazes at it.
The universe quivers during a second of silence
And sleep reclaims its rights,
And the universe resumes its course
Along the millions of white paths traced throughout the world
Across the dark fields.

Les sans cou

In league with saltpeter and mountains, the black ox,
   one eye hidden by a rose, comes to conquer
   the valley, the forest and the land.
Where dandelion flowers make awkward stars in
   the green firmament of sparse grass.
Where rich vivid cow dung, reluctant sunflowers, and
   precious gorse are shining.
Where the wheat is ripe, where clay slashed into cracked branches
   makes gullies for beetles to play in
Where the yellow scorpion loves and dies of love
   lying stiff,
Where the gold-dust sand blinds the tramp.
Moving heavily, swinging his giant head on its furry neck,
   his tail periodically beating its fleshy rump,
The black ox, like ink, looms up, passes by and disappears.
He crushes and marks with his stain the dazzling landscape
While his horns wait for him to pick the right direction
To take sunlight to its death in their orbit open
   to the void,
Heightening the sheen on his glistening hide and,
   with stain flowing from stain, casting
His fantastic shadow on earth thirsting for the next rainfall
And the wavering of butterflies,
Or perhaps a dazzling rose born in the lonely atmosphere
   and growing between the branches of their crescent
   like a phantom flower.

Les sans cou

Come, one Englishman says to another, and the Englishman comes.
Come, says the stationmaster, and the traveler coming to town
    gets off the train suitcase in hand.
Come, somebody else says, and he goes to dinner.
Comme, I say *comme* and everything is changed, marble into water,
    sky orange, wine clear, one thread into six,
    pain in the heart, fear in the belly.
But if the Englishman says *as,* it's his turn to see the world change
    into whatever shape he likes
But I don't see anything more than a particular mark on a card:
The *as* of hearts if it's February
The *as* of diamond-shaped military packs and the *as* of clubs,
    for the misery of Flanders.
The *as* of spades in the hands of adventurers.
And if the spirit moves me I'll say so-and-so to you,
Water jug, muslin, pumpkin.
Let the Englishman say so-and-so.
Let the stationmaster say so-and-so.
Somebody else say so-and-so.
Me too.
And even so-and-so whatchamacallit.
It's true and you don't give a damn.
That you don't know why this poem is the way it is.
Neither do I.
Poem, can I ask you a question?
Poem, can I have a little jelly
And a little lamb to go with it?
And a little glass of wine
Just to get things moving?
Poem, I'm not asking you what time it is.
Poem, I'm not asking if your father-in-law was a tunnel-digger in the
    war.
Poem, what I'm asking for is . . .

Poem, I'm not asking for a handout.
I'm giving you one.
Poem, I'm not asking you what time it is,
I'm telling you.
Poem, I'm not asking if you're doing OK,
That's obvious.
Poem, poem, what I'm asking for is . . .
A little wealth so I can be happy
With the woman I love

Les sans cou

To guess there's a woman walking
Behind a wall spiked with shards of broken bottles
Is an easy game for passersby.
But to guess who drank all those bottles
Before breaking them into a thousand pieces
To guess who drank them all, is a more difficult trick.

To guess there's a woman walking is easy for the passerby.
A parasol distorts her shadow, making it a flower.
A button falls off her dress and is lost in the grass.
One tree abandoned among all others
Counts the tattoos living on its trunk.

But to guess who drank all those bottles,
Boatman full of leaves, that you throw into
The course of rivers and canals
With the words "I love you" and the current carries
Past fishing boats and the danger of dams and locks
To charming villas at the foot of hillsides.

Before smashing them into little pieces
The river comes to see its fish reflected in them
Then ties them up with its murderous plants
And the mermaids of the still waters, supremely treacherous,
Make them ring with a smack from their tails.

But to guess who drank all those bottles is a more difficult trick . . .
It was your mouths, boatmen sleeping on your barges
Sometimes turning slowly and sinking straight down
    in the still waters,
To a hole in the bottom with the perch and the eel,
Down where the bottles don't go.

Some of the pieces were tossed and turned so long
The men who found them thought they must be diamonds.
The wiliest carved magical signs on them
Because they knew the secret of talismen, to make slaves
    of beautiful women
And from that time on their blood flowed between the shores
From that time on the blood of those beautiful women
Selected by the carvers of charms flowed between the shores.
And the fields the cattle returned from to their Savior-less stables
Watched the river flow red between the green hillsides,
And at night were stunned to see the white reflection of the stars.
And the river ended in dark caves,
And its origin destined it for greedy mouths,
And that's why, you boatmen who take this liquid for wine,
You pay the debt of the carvers of charms and the love
    of those beautiful vanished women.
Why, when bloated with that carnal wine, when you've gone straight
     down
    to the bottom of the hole with the perch and the eel
The bottles you shattered
Gleam in the sun's monotonous rays on the wall
Behind which it's easy to guess there's a woman walking
Easy to walk with the woman who can guess.

Les sans cou

Paper, go fold yourself, be a rose and a rainbow,
Be silk, be there this evening,
Be tired.
A forgotten sickle lying beside a dead body slowly opens her eyes,
Sways for a moment, shakes her old-fashioned ruffles,
   and looks at herself in the mirror of her body,
Is shocked, gets furious, goes wild.
The dead man gives her a potato, a very small one,
Which she cuts down
Cuts down the rose the rainbow the silk the evening
Then lies down again beside the corpse.
Unrolling a coil of yarn dirtied by time and dust
   and the water which sweats through old walls,
The sky slips behind a forest where many women
   understand each other, are open, ask questions,
In the thick shadows of tree trunks.
No one comes out of the bizarrely-painted little house at the top of
     the hill,
In spite of the crowd which suddenly appears at the bend in the road,
   red flags flapping in the wind,
Even in spite of their cries: Comrade, Comrade, Comrade,
     COMRADES!
Here's what the countryside was like before the great event:
Several flies buzzed around a cut which steel ran from
   more easily than blood.
The sound of a faraway hammer leaves
Flying with its little straw hat on.
As for the sickle, the odors of the wind show her
   a blue chemise and then a yellow one.
The odors of the river show her a tunic made of coral
   and one made of steel.
The odors of the leaves show her one made of saltpeter and
     phosphorus,

And the odors of the final hour, a satin crinoline
    decorated with flowers.
Twirling her parasol, she waited
Until the sound of the faraway hammer arrived,
Tipping his hat to her,
A bouquet in his hands, with just the hint of a smile.
They ate chicken and drank Pommard,
They ate blackbirds and drank champagne,
They ate oysters and lobster,
Then played loser wins with the women.
They fought like ragpickers
Until the moment when the sky, calm again,
And pleased with their injuries,
Came out from behind the woods.
Is it your fate to be tricked by shadows?
Is it any better to be tricked by the flesh?
To lose blood from endless wounds
And offer death nothing more than a sad feast and poor hospitality?

Les sans cou

Houses with no windows, no doors, with roofs caved in,
Doors without locks,
Guillotine with no blade . . .
I'm talking to you who no longer have ears
Or mouths, noses, eyes, hair, brains
Or heads.
You appear suddenly striding firmly at the bend in the road
    leading to the tavern.
You sit yourselves down, you drink, hard and heavy,
And soon the wine is flowing through your veins,
      bringing new life:
      "What'd you do with your wig?" one headless man
      asks another,
Who looks away without answering
And is dragged out and stomped on.
    "And what's up with you?"
    "I'm the man all laws are drawn up against.
The one extremist parties always call a criminal.
I'm a common-law man
Common as the ovens the bread of our fathers
    was baked in.
I'm the rebel against all civilization,
Abject assassin, vile seducer of little girls, satyr,
Despicable thief.
I'm the traitor and the coward,
Though maybe it takes more courage
To kill in oneself the morals of dumb stories
Than to challenge their belief
(Not a bad form of courage, either).
I'm the one who defies all rules,
The enemy of all lawmakers.
An anarchist? Hardly.
I'm the one the weight of whatever code falls on,

The man with superhuman senses.
I foretell tomorrow's Moses
And tomorrow that Moses exterminates everyone like me,
The eternal victim,
The man without a head,
Now pour me some wine and let's drink a toast."
When he'd finished speaking
It was my turn:
"You have the best wishes of Robert Desnos, Robert le Diable,
    Robert Macaire, Robert Houdini, Robert Robert
    and my uncle Robert,
So sing along with me, all together now, come on you, the little lady
    on my right,
The bearded gent on my left,
One, two, three:
The best of everything from Robert Desnos, Robert le Diable
    Robert Macaire, Robert Houdini, Robert Robert
    and my uncle Robert" . . .
And I haven't included the best of them.
My people, dear headless men,
Men born too soon, forever too soon,
Men who would've been steeled in tomorrow's revolutions
If fate hadn't made you make revolutions to die in.
Men eager for an excess of justice,
In a common grave at the foot of the Mur des Fédères,
In spite of your bullet-hole necklaces.
Men used to fences laid out in the open
Because you don't mix battle-flags with dust rags.
They get nailed to poles
And it's they, the humiliated, that flap so pitifully in the dawn breeze
At the moment when the falling blade
Rings with the echoes of everlasting toasts!

Les sans cou

"My baby," says he and "My baby" says she,
And my blood, our heart, our city, the huge
    frantic city.
Street-workers got lost this morning in fields
    where cornflowers were singing,
Where nightingales bloomed,
Where blah-blah and blah-blah were at the disposal
    of all and sundry.
One guy had a toothache, a backache,
    a noseache.
Lace hung from his nose.
"Baby, is this our life? Is it all over?
It seems so empty and hollow even dull
    and so forth.
I feel your blood running through my hands,
And April isn't over on New Year's Eve!"

"Deep in snow the knight-of-sidewalks goes nuts with joy,
Sleeps, dreams, yells out
Morning baby and you too baby
And same to your back your belly and your mouth.
On your feet street-walker, dumbbell, phony-of-phonies."
The night I'm talking about is a twenty-four hour one.
The anchor drops with a loud noise into a bottomless swamp
Into so many foul memories and so many foul years
And this damned month of April
That isn't over on New Year's Eve!
January loses its shirt,
And July its shoe.
Everything old, decaying, shameful, shabby, snot-nosed
And this god-damned month of April
Which isn't over, and never will be,
Even on New Year's Eve!

Les sans cou

Where are you headed, you bunch of fakes?
Where are you going, for Chrissake?
With asses for brains
And dollar-signs for hearts?

We're going to piss in the clover,
spit in the hay.

Where are you going with asses for brains?
Where are you going with all this fuss?
The sun looks a little thin,
Just a little thin tonight.
Where are you going, money-on-the-brains?

We're going to piss in the clover,
spit in the hay.

Where, where are you going
In the mud and the dark?
We're going to spit in the clover,
piss in the hay.
Like a bunch of idiots,
Hare-lipping along,
We're going to piss in the clover.

Wait, I'm coming too.
Full speed ahead: I'll catch up to you.
You clowns, my buddies,
I'm going to piss in the clover,
spit in the hay.

But why aren't you coming along?
I'm not coming along, I'm even getting better.

You clown-hearts and lion-balls!
I'm coming to piss, piss with you
In the clover
And spit in the hay.
In those kisses after midnight, you can taste the rust,
the iron, the man.
You taste! You taste the woman!
And lots of other things too:
the pen-holder you chewed when you were four
And just learning to write,
The new notebooks, the books you got as gifts,
All gilt and red
That sticks and bleeds on your fingertips.
Kisses after midnight,
Swimming in streams cold
As a razor's edge.

Les sans cou

THE SATYR

Out of the dark at last,
And out of the mud.
God! The way they stick to the feet and the limbs!
This path leads to clear waters where people swim
   between the grassy banks.
Shadowy waters,
Grazed by wingtips.
Pure water, wash me clean.
I give myself to your flow where leaves
   brought down by the wind still green go sailing along.
Pure water endlessly washing reflections.
Pure water shivering in the wind,
I'll wash and leave mine with you!
You can wash that image I don't want to see myself in,
Or carry it far away,
Where the ocean will dissolve it like salt.
Off with the jacket, the collar and tie, awful uniform
   of the dull life I lead.
Feet leaping out of the heavy shoes,
Pants sliding down my legs,
The feel of the cloth.
Ah! the cool wind, the shirt shooting out suddenly
Like sperm or champagne.
And that flash of skin glimpsed naked in the sun.
The hair bristling like grass
Where the huge flower of the sex blooms in the shadow
   of the thighs.
The rush of air in the dark stinking corridors
   of the flesh,
Cheeks exposed, luminous, like the body of a nymph . . .
Withered, pimply, flesh as colorless as my life.
And, deep inside me, the longing for a lonely shepherdess or a princess
   is born and rises like nausea.

Once I had flowers in my hands,
In my mouth the juice of flowers and grass and sap and sand
    even the soaking-wet soil of marshes,
A sweet bitterness the wind added its own to
    filled my mouth.
My body was covered with pollen.
I could taste the meadow, the river, the forests full of fern
    and mushroom.
I walked in earth
Up to my knees, up to my sex, my navel,
    my mouth and my eyes.
So what? Alone here in the shade . . .
My solitude is filled with phantom creatures of my sexuality.
What a crowd! What chaos!

This is the satyr talking.
His suspenders already drooping in a sordid way.
This is him talking.
Is he really himself or has he merged with
    that cast of characters?
But first a word about his decor:
The wall filled with passionate graffiti,
Where at twilight he pastes his shadow like a poster
Wall oozing with the piss of dogs and men,
The wall he turns away from, as if surprised,
Where, fired by invisible guns, images of himself
    pile up and stink.
Then the toilet, dimly-lit
By stained glass,
Filled with the song of fountains,
Fragrant, slit like a blockhouse,
Its only entrance onto the noisy street.

Then there's the forest . . .
Studded with obscene mushrooms,
Thick with fleshy blooms,

114   Smelling of a thousand odors of crime, betrayal, shame,
and mystery.
At the base of a tree, one evening while bells are ringing
on the plain,
A desperate man commits suicide.
In the shadow of a bush, two lovers merge.
In a brook, dead leaf and uprooted grass sail by.
Bird tracks are printed in the mud.
Initials carved on oaks lose meaning year by year.
Hazelnuts ripen under the leaves,
Noise in the burrows.
Morel and chanterelle are born, live and die.
And finally there's you, satyr,
Watching for headlights
In the night
So you can expose yourself at the edge of the road
Or be caught in an obscene pose
At a bend in the path.

Ah! let the deer in the valley be belled . . .
So the last earthly sound you hear
Echoing in your skull is a shot fired by a clumsy hunter
Wasting his ammunition.

Ragged priests have thrown away the cloth here
And suddenly you recognize the dirty shiver of confessions,
Murmur of invented sins,
And the gulf that separates your unchained dreams
And the huge belly ripped open by a knife
Inviting you to probe the sticky pile of guts.

No!
The satyr's dreaming and rolling in the golden dung
of his imagination.
Faced with its reality,
Zeal, genitals and desire

Shrink.
Betrayed by the weakness of his flesh
The satyr disappears
Dissolves
Runs away
Vanishes.
And the only thing left
Lost in a field of sparrows
The robes of a scarecrow castrated,
Gutted like a rabbit,
Swollen by a distant wind
Coming from some other place
Like a dream of love or thought
Swollen by a distant wind,
After it's dried the love-stained sheets,
Seeded cesspools and shitpiles
With grass and strange flowers.
A windbag scarecrow that doesn't even frighten
    birds or children.
Childish like a game of marbles,
Like the secret universe
Of every man,
And absurd and logical like a game of marbles,
Is the satyr who approaches you in the shadows
Violently piling up then trampling
His tumultuous dreams.

Fortunes

That bellowing in the black street at whose end
the river shudders against its banks.
That butt thrown from a window forms a star.
That bellowing again in the black street.
Ah! Shut your traps!
Oppressive, stifling night.
A cry approaches, almost touching,
but dies at the very moment it reaches us.

Somewhere in the world, at the foot of an embankment,
a deserter pleads with sentries
who do not understand his language.

Les portes battantes

Four of us were at a table
Drinking red wine and singing
As we pleased.

A wallflower fades in a garden gone to seed
The memory of a dress at the bend of an avenue
Venetian blinds beating against a sash.

The first man says: "The world is wide and the wine is fine
Wide is my heart and fine my blood
Why are my hands and my heart so empty?"

A summer evening the chants of rowers on a river
The reflection of huge poplars
And the foghorn of a tug requesting passage.

The second man says: "I discovered a fountain
The water was fresh and sweet-smelling
I no longer know where it is and all four of us are dying."

How beautiful are the streams in small towns
On an April morning
When they carry rainbows along.

The third man says: "We were born a short time ago
And already we have more than a few memories
Though I want to forget them."

A stairway full of shadow
A door left ajar
A woman surprised naked.

118   The fourth man says: "What memories?
At this moment we're camped
And friends we're going to leave each other."

Night falls on a crossroad
The first light in the fields
The odor of burning grass.

We left each other, all four of us
Which one was I and what did I say?
It was a long long time ago.

The glistening rump of a horse
The cry of a bird in the night
The rippling of water under a bridge.

One of the four is dead
Two others are hardly better off
But I'm doing well and I think it'll last a long while.

The hillsides covered with thyme
The ancient mossy courtyard
The old street that led to the forest.

Men, life, friendships reborn,
And the blood of the whole world circulating in veins,
In many different veins but in the veins of men,
   of men on earth.

Les portes battantes

Iron anemone sheet.

A spear's iron pierces the anemone, which bleeds on the sheet.

Iron stained with the blood of anemones whiteness of sheets.

Iron in the heart anemone in the wound winding sheet

Iron anemone sheet.

And that sheet reddened by anemone blood hangs from
    the iron shaft

And the sheet wipes the iron that gashed the anemone.

Throw away the faded anemone.

The iron and the sheet remain.

Throw away the rusty iron!

The sheet remains.

The sheet that will take longer to rot than the body it wraps.

The sheet that won't leave its skeleton remains.

Throw away the sheet!

Get back the iron!

Pick the anemone!

The flesh around the iron of your skeleton:

Your body

A red flag folded back up.

Les portes battantes

Once there was a leaf with its lines
Life line
Luck line
Heart line
Once there was a branch at the end of the leaf
Forked line life sign
Luck sign
Heart sign
Once there was a tree at the end of the branch
A tree worthy of life
Worthy of luck
Heart worthy
Heart carved, pierced through and through
A tree no one ever saw.
There were roots at the end of the tree
Roots life-vines
Luck vines
Heart vines
At the end of the roots the earth
The earth, period
The earth too-round
The earth all alone crossing the sky
The earth.

Les portes battantes

At the bend in the road
He reached out
To the beautiful morning.

The sky was so clear
The clouds looked
Like foam on the sea.

And blossoms on the apple trees
Turned white in meadows
Where wash was hung out to dry.

The spring which sang
Sang of the life which passed
Along the meadows and the hedgerows.

And the distant forest
Where the grass was turning green
Was full of bell-like sounds.

Life was so beautiful
It entered his eyes
His heart and his ears so completely,

That he broke out laughing:
He laughed at the world and at the sighing
Wind in the flowering trees.

He laughed at the way the earth smelled,
He laughed at the wash of the washerwomen,
He laughed at the clouds passing overhead.

As he was laughing on a hilltop,
A girl with a beautiful face appeared
From a house nearby.

And the girl laughed too
And when her laughter vanished
The birds began to sing again.

She laughed to see him laugh
And the doves mirrored
In the still waters of a pond
Heard her laughter vanish in the air.

They never saw each other again.

She often went along the road
Where the man held out his hand
To the morning light.

Many times he remembered her
And the all too clear memory
Could be seen in his eyes.

Many times she remembered him
And saw his face
In the dark water of a well.

One by one the years passed
Turning pale like the cards a player holds
In his hand as dawn breaks.

Both are rotting in the earth
Chewed by the honest worms.
The earth fills their mouths to keep them quiet.

They might call out to each other at night
If death weren't so horrified by the sound:
The road is there and time passes.

But every day a beautiful morning
Falls like an egg into the hand
Of someone passing along the road.

Every day the sky is so clear
That the clouds
Are like foam on the sea.

Dead people! Dark wrecks in the earth,
We don't know your miseries
The hermits sing of.

We swim, we are alive,
In the innocent air of each season.
Life is beautiful and the air is good.

Les portes battantes

Today I took a walk with my friend
Even though he's dead,
I took a walk with my friend.

How beautiful the flowering trees,
The chestnut trees that snowed the day he died.
With my friend I took a walk.

Long ago my parents
Went to funerals alone
And I felt like a little child.

Now I know a good many dead men
I've seen a lot of undertakers
But I don't get too close to them.

That's why all day today
I took a walk with my friend.
He found me aged a little,

Aged a little, but he said:
Someday you too will be where I am,
One Saturday or Sunday.

And I looked at the flowering trees,
At the river passing under the bridge
And suddenly saw I was alone.

So I came back among the living.

État de veille

Day after day
Wave after wave
Where are you going? Where are you going?
Earth wounded by so many wandering men!
Earth fertilized by the bodies of so many.
But the earth is us,
We're not on it
We're in it for all time—

État de veille

AT FIVE O'CLOCK

At five o'clock in the morning in a new and empty street
    I hear the sound of a car driving off.
A fire alarm box has a broken window and the shards
    of glass are shining in the gutter.

On the pavement there is a puddle of blood and a puff of smoke
    vanishes in the air.
You there! Wait! tell me what happened.
Wake up! I want to know what happened.
Tell me what happens in the lives of men.

1936

État de veille

Then the trumpet will sound at the city gates
And birds will fly off at the sound of the brass
They will soar above the city for a long time
And when they come to rest
We'll already be resting
Merry, joyful, fulfilled of heart,
Sleeping in the night before the first dawn
    of returning happiness.

1936

État de veille

We'll laugh about it later
But for now we don't cry about it
Cascades of flowers and liqueurs
Enormous abscess of perfumes
Geyser of sap and water
Everything under our eyes in the earth springs like milk
    from the udder in the fingers of the farmer's wife
The grape ripens and from the grape will gush the geyser-of-wine
The acorn sprouts, and from the acorn the oak will spray a geyser
    of leaves and songs
The sea rises and falls and from her foam the wreck
    and the unknown continent, geyser of wood, of earth and
    old seaweed, are spat
And what?
We'd only dream a hole in this generous earth
We'd only dream death in this world where life
    is offered us
We'd only dream a death that doesn't exist in this
    world where so many things are beautiful
Where all could be beautiful
Where it feels good to live and to live forever.

Mines de rien

You take the first street to the right
You follow the wharf
You pass the bridge
You knock at the door.

The sun shines
The river runs
At a window a pot of geraniums trembles
A car crosses over to the other bank.

You return to yourself in this merry landscape
Without noticing that the door is open behind you
The hostess stands at the doorway
The house is filled with shadows.

But on the table you notice a reflection
The reflection of day on fruit and on a bottle
On an earthenware plate and a piece of furniture
And you remain there on the doorstep between
The world full of people like yourself
And your droning isolation from the rest of the world.

undated.

Poètes d'aujourd'hui. "Robert Desnos," by Pierre Berger.

SONG FOR THE
BEAUTIFUL SEASON

Nothing looks more like inspiration
Than the drunkenness of a spring morning,
Than the desire for a woman.
No longer to be oneself, but to be each one.
To set your feet on the earth nimbly.
To savor the air you breathe.

This evening I'm singing not of what we must fight against
But of what we must defend.
The pleasures of life.
The wine drunk with comrades.
Love.
The fire in winter.
The cool river in summer.
The meat and bread of each meal.
The refrain you sing while walking down the road.
The bed you sleep in.
The sleep without sudden waking, without anguish for the next day.

Leisure.
The freedom to change one's sky.
The feeling of dignity and many other things
Some dare refuse men possession of.

I love and I sing the blossoming spring.
I love and I sing the summer with its fruits.
I love and I sing the joy of living.
I love and I sing the spring.
I love and I sing the summer, season of my birth.

Mines de rien

Hail, coming harvests, scented, bloody,
    intoxicating harvests of the coming autumn
Hail, groaning winepresses, echoing barrels,
    bung holes, cellars, hail

Hail bottles, corks, and glasses
Hail drinkers of future years
Drinkers who'll drink greedily
Drinkers who'll drink learnedly

I'll drink this wine that matures in the green grapes of this wonderful
    spring 1938 with gay companions
With you Jean-Louis Barrault for whom there is no wine
    but Burgundy
With you, old Carp, easily seduced by Algerian vintages
With Fraenkel, no hater of Bordeaux
With you, Youki, who appreciate Champagne
I'll drink this wine of the coming harvest
Until there isn't a drop left in any cellar
    even one forgotten in the bottom of a flask
I'll drink trusting in life loving life with all my
    heart
Unable to stop loving it
Even if like a woman
It cheats or abandons me.

1937–1938

Mines de rien

FIRE

And from the shores of the ocean to the Mediterranean
     a tide of fires surged, of smoke and blood
Fire and blood
They all rose up in the cities and in the villages
     on the rocky mountainsides emaciated like
     the dead
Fire and blood and death
They fought and this word, only Freedom,
Floated in the sound of battles, cried out by the best of us,
     and the flower of the youth of the world, of the free youth
     of the world
friend from Mexico, Tata Nacho, isn't it right that we
     are elbow to elbow with Spain
friend from Russia, Eisenstein,
All heart to heart with Spain
friends from the United States, Hemingway, Dos Passos,
and you, Shipman, more passionate than anyone else
friend from Chile, Cotapos, you the most joyous of all
friend from Guatemala, Asturias, all irony and sentiment
friend from Cuba, Felix de Castro, the flame and its warmth
friends, friends from all countries
All heart to heart with Spain
friend from Norway, Per Krogh, the loyalty, the rectitude,
     and the courage
eye to eye, heart to heart with Spain
which triumphs at the moment I write these lines
friend from India, Charles Baron, too tender too friendly
friend by the liver fired by alcohol and the faith fired by doubt,

     but in the hand of our Spanish brothers
friend of Japan, the only one maybe, Takasaki, large eyes
     open, clumsy mouth, eyes henceforth closed,
     mouth closed, Takasaki, dead for all the years you
     would've been with us for Spain For Republican Spain.

Mines de rien

AFTERWORD TO
ÉTAT DE VEILLE

The first poems of this volume date from 1936. During that entire year
and until spring of 1937, I forced myself to write a poem each evening,
before falling asleep. With or without a subject, tired or not, I faithfully
observed this discipline. In this way I filled a series of notebooks in
which, you can imagine, I found many rejects when I began to reread
the poems in 1940. Some, somehow, are in *Fortunes* under the general
title of *Les portes battantes.* The following poems are not published in
their original form. They have sometimes been completely revised. But
the experience of writing them was worthwhile. Some evenings the
poem would come on its own, having constructed itself during the
course of the day. Other times with an empty mind, it was an
unexpected theme that would guide the hand rather than thought. But
it was not automatic writing. Each word, each verse was controlled,
and the mechanical demand would manifest itself rather in the rhythm,
in the necessity of assonance and of primitive forms such as rhymed
tercets. The result of such an enterprise was a complete intellectual
"purge" that would definitely have made me give up poetry if I had not
had the luck at the time to be one of the most productive slogan
writers and radio publicity announcers.

All free poetic substance, all inspiration long consumed, I spent
my time working passionately on the almost mathematical but still
intuitive work of adapting words to music and of making sentences,
proverbs, and publicity slogans—work whose first demand was a
return to the popular rules in terms of rhyme. I don't doubt that one
day the folklorists will examine the enormous commercial production
of the various French radio stations during that time and find a pretext
to teach about the French sensibility and way of life.

I built upon this "forced poem" of "verses"—composed with the
ambition to propose to musicians texts resembling Spanish "couplets,"
Cuban "sounds," or American "blues." They could use these with the
greatest freedom—in cutting, in repetition of sentences, even in adding
what they would like to add, with the hope that they would extend to
the orchestras the same freedom for the execution of their music.

Poems more classical in appearance complete this volume. They are part of a continuing experience, the evolution of which it is impossible to predict and of which I can't speak clearly.

It is enough to say that I try to go back to Nerval, maybe also to Gongora, or rather to start again from their work by different paths than those that led the poetry across such shifting landscapes up to the perhaps too cultivated field of the present.

Finally, it is not poetry that has to be free, it is the poet.

Tonight the toothless camel
Is not happy.
It went to the dentist,
A sad dark man,
And the dentist said
That his treatment was not for him.
Bunch of bastards, the camel said,
You came here on my sands
With unfriendly airs,
Airs of desert, of course,
And sour as sour apples.
You put a saddle on me
And rode me under your canopy
So go fuck yourself
If I have a toothache . . .
But you have no more teeth!
Well exactly, my teeth ache because I have none.
So, do you want false teeth?
I'd like to see a camel with a set of false teeth!
A set of false choppers chomping at the bit!
The camel has no more teeth,
He has been deserted in the desert.
So he slowly pisses in the sand that sinks into a funnel
While the caravan draws further away, through the dunes sunk into
      funnels,
Through the dunes
Themselves sunk into funnels.

État de veille

TALE OF A BEAR

A bear made her way into the city.
She walked heavily
And waterdrops shone in her fur
Like diamonds.

She walked unrecognized
Through the streets
In her furry coat.

The crowd went by.
No one watched her.
She was even jostled.

At last, night fell to its knees
Letting its red hair stream
Into streams of mud,

In the sea longing for its tides
In the meadows, in the forests,
And in the lighted cities.

The bear was sucked into the multitude
Into the crowd, into the shadows
Mingled with ruins.

Only a few astronomers
Lying in wait under domes
Saw her spirit pass.

You will be called The Great Bear
As you follow your course
To light and its source.

You will be adorned with stars
And from the depths of their jail
Prisoners will see you pass across their air hole.

Bear whatever, bear of feather,
Roaring Bear slavering with foam
Sparking more than a hammer striking an anvil,

Bear whatever, the tale
And your trail on the sand
Fraying like an old cable.

I hear heavy steps in the night
I hear songs and shouts
The shouts and songs of my friends.

Their steps are heard
But when day comes
Freedom and love will be born.

It will be made of light and blood
And it will replenish the four elements
Whether it's born tomorrow or in a hundred years.

Heavier than the bear in the city
Throughout the world I sense the rising
Of the great invasion, the great tide.

Great Bear you're shining
In the night sky as I listen for
The cries, for the songs of my friends.

État de veille

VERSE ON THE PORTES SAINT-MARTIN AND SAINT-DENIS

Porte Saint-Martin, Porte Saint-Denis,
To see the moon shine through the arch,
Porte Saint-Martin, Porte Saint-Denis,
From north to south the road stretches,
Porte Saint-Martin, Porte Saint-Denis,
To walk under the arch at daybreak,
Porte Saint-Martin, Porte Saint-Denis,
To sip black coffee with friends,
Porte Saint-Martin, Porte Saint-Denis,
When the sky turns white at dawn,
Porte Saint-Martin, Porte Saint-Denis,
To drown your oldest sorrows in the dawn,
To leave singing toward a far-off goal,
With our buddies, with our friends,
Porte Saint-Denis, Porte Saint-Martin,
To leave singing in a lovely morning.

1942

État de veille

VERSES ON
RUE SAINT-MARTIN

I don't like rue Saint-Martin anymore
Since André Platard left it.
I don't like rue Saint-Martin anymore,
I don't like anything, not even wine.

I don't like rue Saint-Martin anymore
Since André Platard left it.
He's my friend, he's my buddy
We shared bread and board.
I don't like the rue Saint-Martin anymore.

He's my friend, he's my buddy.
He disappeared one morning,
They took him away with them, no one knows anything.
He's never been seen again on rue Saint-Martin.

No use praying to the saints,
Saints Merri, Jacques, Gervais, and Martin,
Not even Valerien hiding on the hill.
Time goes by, no one knows anything.
André Platard left the rue Saint-Martin.

1942

État de veille

VERSE ON THE
RUE DE BAGNOLET

The Sun of the rue de Bagnolet
Is not a sun like the others.
It bathes in the gutter,
It wears a bucket on its head,
Just like the others,
But, it touches my shoulders,
It's really it and not another,
The sun of the rue de Bagnolet
Which drives its horse cart
Somewhere else than to the palace gates,
Sun, sun neither beautiful nor ugly,
Sun quite funny and quite content,
Sun of the rue de Bagnolet,
Sun of winter and spring,
Sun of the rue de Bagnolet,
Not like the others.

1942

État de veille

VERSE ON THE
SUMMERTIME SIDEWALK

Let's lie down on the paving stones,
Warmed and washed by the sun,
In the good smell of dust
When day is over,
Before night falls,
Before first light
And we'll watch in the stream
For the reflections of clouds building,
The blush of the horizon
And the first star above the houses.

1942

État de veille

VERSE ON THE GLASS OF WINE

When the train leaves don't wave
Your hand, your handkerchief, or your parasol
But rather fill a glass of wine
And toss the long flame of wine
toward the train whose slatted sides are singing
The bloody flame of wine like your tongue
And share with it
The palace and the bed
Of your lips and your mouth.

1942

État de veille

Lovely one, if you wish, I'll make your bed
In the bloody setting of my shop.
My knives will be the magic mirrors
Where day breaks, shines, and pales.

I will make your hollow and warm bed
In the open womb of a heifer
As you sleep may it make you young again
I will watch over it like a hangman over a scaffold.

1942

État de veille

TOMORROW

A hundred thousand years old, I would still have the strength
To wait for you, o tomorrow, premonition of hope.
Time, an old man suffering from multiple ailments,
May moan: The morning is new, new the evening.

But for too many months we have been living at the brink,
We stay awake, keep watch over light and fire,
We speak in whispers and strain our ears
At many sounds muffled and lost as in a game.

Meanwhile, from the depths of night we still witness
The splendor of the day and all its gifts.
If we do not sleep, it is to watch for the dawn,
Which will prove that at last we are living in the present.

1942

État de veille

The day is as it should be and flows with the fullness of time,
Unless a being rises through the spaces
Superimposed on memory and relieving
Thought and the heart of stubborn recollections.

Summers, potent summers, even your name passes,
To be and to have been, time past and springtime,
It passes, it is past, like a never weary stream,
Without scars, without witnesses and without ponds.

Seasons, at least you cherish the grain of wheat
That sprouts in the spring thaw and is the key
To open the porte cochere when it's time to leave.

The stars in the sky are assembled by you,
The year is going to end soon and heavy steps
Drag on the paths returning to the borders.

1942

État de veille

Across the snout
Picked up in the mud and slime
Spit out, vomited, rejected—
I am the verse witness of my master's breath—
Left over, cast off, garbage
Like the diamond, the flame, and the blue of sky
Not pure, not virgin
But fucked to the core
fucked, pricked, sucked, ass fucked, raped
I am the verse witness of my master's breath
Fucker and violator
Not a maiden
There's nothing dirtier than virginity
Ouf! Here today gone tomorrow
Good muddy earth where I set my foot
I ride the wind, the great wind and the sea
I am the verse witness of my master's breath
That cracks farts sings snores
Great storm-wind heart of the world
There is no longer a foul weather
I love all the weathers I love the time
I love the high wind
The great wind the rain the screams the snow the sun the fire and
all that is earth muddy or dry
And let it collapse!
And let it rot!
Rot old flesh old bones
Across the snout
And let it break your teeth and make your gums bleed
I am the verse witness of my master's breath
The water is running with its absurd hummingbird song
of nightingale and alchohol burning in a saucepan
running down my body

A mushroom rots in the corner of a dark forest
   where an incredibly beautiful woman is lost, sloshing in bare feet
There's something rotting at the oak roots
A gold medal couldn't resist it
It's mushy
It's deep
It gives in
There's something rotting at the oak roots
A moon from long ago
Is reflected in this rot
Smell of death smell of life of embrace
Comical shadow-creatures must be rolling
struggling and kissing here
There's something rotting at the oak roots
And it blows even worse at the summit
Nests shaken and the famous hummingbird from before
Rushed
Hoarse nightingales
Foliage of the immense and fluttering forests
Soiled and crumbled like shit-house paper
Hellish and high tides from the summit
of the forests your waves draw toward the sky
The fleshy hills in a foam
of clearings and pastures veined by
rivers and minerals
At last here he comes out of his cave
The skinned-alive one who sings with his throat slit
No nails at the end of his fingers
Orpheus is his name
Cold-blooded fucker, confidant of the Sibyls
A Bacchus eunuch delirious and clairvoyant
A man once of good earth and come from good seed by
   good wind
Speaks, bleeds, and keels over
Broken teeth split kidneys knotted arteries
Worthless heart

148   While the river flows rolls and makes
       the grotesque wreckage of houseboats drunk
       coal flowing from them
       Reaches the plain and reaches the sea
       froths rolls and soaks into
       the sand the salt and the coral
       I will come into your waves
       After the worn-out river
       Watch out for your fleet
       Watch out for your coral, your sand, your salt for your feasts
       Come out of the walls with passwords
       Out of snouts
       Across teeth
       Good weather
       For the men worthy of this name
       Good weather for rivers and trees
       Good weather for the sea
       The froth and the mud remain
       And the joy of living
       And one hand in mine
       And the joy of living
       I am the verse witness of my master's breath.

       Sens

Summer dusk bathed in rose mist
Torn by the blue of roof slates,
The blue of sky, the blue of asphalt, and, sometimes,
Bleeding on a window where reflections collide

The river's reflection captured in foliage
The reflection of sound, the reflection of a rumpled bed,
The trembling of panes at the convoys roaring past,
Everything here meets and transforms itself.

The sun rolls heavily over the houses,
In the murmur of evening and the echo of songs:
Night will erase this fragile universe,

The ghost of a bed abandoned by lovers
And the flaw in glass imitating a diamond
But the window will go on trembling over the city.

Sens

WINDOW

Through a golden yellow window
The apple and the pineapple enter
The insect and the fish
The bird and the shadow

Don't make such a fuss
Over a dish of exotic vegetables
The boat sailing out of another age
Will make it safely to port

To safe port and to be at their mercy
To safe port and despite everything
A scream never having broken four legs
Of an armchair.

Sens

At the bend of the mountain pass
The carcass of the mule dead since last year
Under the too heavy burden he was carrying
Is turning white under the blazing sun.

The perfume of thyme and the buzzing of insects
Are enough to drug a passerby
Who senses time hesitating to follow its path
And the world wavering in the heat.

In the valley at the foot of steep hills
Mules are trotting by
To the sound of their bells and shoes.

In the barnyard some men surround
A sheep that just gave birth
And one of them raises a lamb to the sky surprised to be alive.

Sens

If Phaedra, after her death, finds you again, Hippolyte,
Both of you having ceased to live at the same time,
What kisses, what embrace beyond the doors of time
Beyond space! . . . A cry transports you and dwells in you.

In the labyrinth, then, of unusual stars,
It is the flight of a bird that wavers bearing
An arrow stuck in its chest, and even so,
This bird restores your color and life with its own blood.

Farewell memory, farewell beautiful names of your loves,
Beautiful senses, farewell. Be mute, blind, deaf,
Mourn with regret your scattered bodies.

The monster is decay and the sky is overcast,
Theseus, on the headland, is fixed in his pose.
Phaedra, your memory weds him to his amazement.

Sens

It's the call from the village to the lazy shepherds
That sings this morning in my heart, and now
That all the glasses are emptied, I long to sleep in the orchards
Where the birds sing, where the bees spin.

Facing the sky and looking into the flying clouds
Giants knocked out by the cold and the night,
I would see tunnels and arches dug out
And dimly lit trees bearing glimmers of fruit.

At the very pit of a crater weighted with vertigos
The star appeared with its crystal points
The morning rose detached from her stem
The pretty walker with her unparalleled looks

Dress of black velvet and brilliant tiara
Mud from a comet on the silk of her blouse
Broken necklace letting so many diamonds fall
That the grass around me weeps

I lock you up in my eyes closed on your beautiful image
At the dark gardens whipped by lightning
That your dress and your feet leave on their passage
When you come out of the tumultuous sea of air.

But I would like to know where you spent the night.
Like me, you sleep in the daylight hours
Indifferent to cries, songs, daylight, noises,
Like me, you are the last to sleep and dream.

And I want to sleep under your net
To see you appear above the countryside
In an orchard loud with bees and birds
In the shade of the tallest castle in Spain

And I'd be dissolved in a deep sleep
Like black coffee and a migraine
In the bronze sonority of the great bell
And the monotony of fire and fountains.

While you, paled by the froth of day,
Would disappear from the sky like a trace of powder
On a face captured by the charms of love
Which flames and rises with the crack of lightning.

Sens

Every day time with its sharp teeth
Tears a little of this mirror's
Patina and to emptiness
Returns its spoils

Leprosy marks its face
And masks the hour's lateness dying out
Weary and weary of recognizing itself
Each night and day

The landscape appears
With its sky and distance
Freeing a reflection that invites
Narcissus to live the uncertain
Limpid, beautiful journey
Between night and day

Sens

She is born at the wane of autumn
She lives in dream all winter
She wakes with a start in the spring
She loves, she loves in full summer

She sows memories in autumn
She forgets memories in winter
She sings life in spring
She's silent, she's silent in summer

She talks through the autumn
She listens to one voice in winter
She goes toward life in spring
She denies, she denies death in summer

You lose track of her in autumn
You forget her, you forget her in winter
Someone remembers her one day in spring
Her name forever lost in the heart of summer

    Autumn, winter, spring, summer
       To be, to be, and to have been

1943

Sens

Eusebe has fertilized his garden
With Pegasus shit
With Pegasus shit?
Oh! oh!
For a shit, what a shit!
Eusebe is hot shit.

Eusebe has fertilized his garden
With Unicorn shit
With Unicorn shit?
Oh! oh!
For a shit, what a shit!
Eusebe is no fool.

Eusebe has fertilized his garden
With Minotaur shit
yeah, Minotaur shit!
oh! oh!
not shit but bullshit
Eusebe put on his lawn.

4 April 1944
Desnos for his friend Eirisch
Compiègne Camp

Sens

SPRING

You, Rrose Selavy, wander out of reach
In the spring caught up in love's sweat,
In the scent of the rose budding on tower walls,
in the ferment of waters and earth.

Bleeding, a rose in his side, the dancer's stone body
Appears in the theater in the midst of ploughing
A mute, blind, and deaf people
will applaud his dance and his spring death.

It is said. But the word written in soot
Is erased by the whims of the winds under fingers of rain
Though we hear and obey it.

At the wash house, where the water runs, a cloud pretends to be
the soap and the storm as it pushes back the moment
when the sun will break the bushes into flower.

Desnos
6–4–44
19, rue Mazarine
Paris VI

Sens

IF, LIKE THE WINDS DRAWN
ON THE COMPASS FACE

If, like the winds drawn on the compass face
There is a meaning to time and space,
If they have one they have a thousand and more
And as many if they don't have any.

For who among us does not imagine or sense
Shadows wandering out of geometries,
Universes eluding our senses?

At the intersections of oblique roads
We listen to a hunter's horn dying out,
Always sounding again, always the same.

This vision of the sky and the compass face
Is absorbed and dissolved in air
Like the sounds that make our flesh quiver
Or the faint lights beneath our closed eyes.

We collide into other universes
Without feeling, seeing, or hearing them
At the depth of summer, at the peak of winter,
The other seasons fall on us in ashes.

While like the winds drawn on the compass face
The door slams and the flags slap,
The sails swell and without visible cause
An absurd presence imposes itself on us
Material, indifferent, and without rest.

Ce coeur qui haïssait la guerre

This heart that hated war is now beating for the struggle.

This heart that once beat only to the rhythm of the tides, the seasons, and the hours of day and night.

Now this heart swells and sends a boiling blood of saltpeter and hate to the veins

And it sends such a hard left to the jaw that the ears whistle

And it's not possible this sound doesn't spread to the town and the countryside

Like a bell tolling for a riot and fight. Listen, I can hear it echoing back to me.

But no, it's the sound of other hearts, of millions of other hearts beating like mine across France.

They beat to the same rhythm for the same task all those hearts,

Their sound is the sea attacking cliffs

And all this blood carries in millions of minds the same watchword:

Rise up against Hitler and death to his partisans!

Nevertheless this heart that hated war once beat to the rhythm of the seasons

But a single word, Freedom, was enough to awaken the old angers

And millions of Frenchmen are preparing in the dark for the work the coming dawn will impose on them

Because these hearts that once hated war beat for liberty to the rhythm of the seasons and the tides, of day and night.

L'Honneur des poètes

And here, Father Hugo, is your name on the walls!
You'd turn over in the grave of the Pantheon
If you knew who did it . . . Who did it? Someone.
Someone is Hitler, Someone is Goebbels . . . The riffraff,

A Laval, a Pétain, a Bonnard, a Brinon,
Those who know how to betray and those who make merry
Those who are destined for just reprisals
And there aren't many names.

These people of little wit and weak culture
Have a need for alibis in their dirty game.
They said, "The guy is dead. He's broken."

Yes, the guy is dead. But in the presence of a lawyer
He made his last will very clear.
The lawyer has a name: France; and the legacy: Freedom.

L'Honneur des poètes

TO CONQUER THE DAY, TO CONQUER THE NIGHT

To conquer the day, to conquer the night
To conquer time that clings to me,
All that silence, all that noise,
My hunger, my fate, my horrible chill.

To defeat this heart, to lay it bare,
To crush this body full of stories
Plunging it into the unknown,
Into the insensible, into the impenetrable.

To break at last, to throw these old idols
To the darkness of sewers
To convert hatred into hope,
Foul words into holy ones.

But isn't my time wasted?
Paris, you took all my blood.
I am the hanged man on your neck
This libertarian who weeps and laughs.

Ce coeur qui haïssait la guerre

The taboo is on you, the taboo is on us! So sing the heroes who are
following you.

The taboo is on you and no one will dare to touch you. Your life is
sacred and you strike fear in killers.

The taboo is on you, the taboo is on us, because we have revived
ancient customs and old ways.

The taboo is on you and we only want to be your barbaric throng,
obeying your orders and dying without a word.

The taboo is on you, the taboo is on us, and it's why we have widened
our circle on earth around you.

The taboo is on you! Our conquests, our bloody sacrifices, are the
measure of our common madness, yours and ours.

The taboo is on you, the taboo is on us! Everywhere we go we
dig our graves instead of our cornerstones.

The taboo is on you and no one can do anything against you, o chief!
o untouchable! like the demented, like lepers and pest carriers.

The taboo is on you, the taboo is on us! An extraordinary death is
keeping us alone in its stables and slaughterhouses.

The taboo is on you, o chief! o gravedigger! and your people march to
your cries toward the inexorable sacrifice.

The taboo is on you, the taboo is on us. The food you refuse to give us
we cannot give to you.

The taboo is on you, and you will starve, like ourselves, following the rite, and the people of the earth will rejoice.

The taboo is on you, the taboo is on us, cruel beasts, mindless killers.

The taboo is on you! Adolf Hitler! Führer!
Chief! The very fate of a people who chose to be criminal and hated.

The taboo is on you, the taboo is on us! And so sing the soldiers of agonizing Germany, mouths of brutes, minds of monkeys, hearts of pigs of agonizing Germany.

The taboo is on you, the taboo is on us! Nothing can free us from the tragic destiny that we have chosen in you, we, the demented German crowd and we who doubt we are alive, and we who are hungry vampires in search of rot and nothingness.

The taboo, the taboo is on you, the taboo is on us and the fall and the death, the defeat and the hunger, with not even a story of gold and blood to draw our shadows from their torment. The taboo is on you, the taboo is on us.

Ce coeur qui haïssait la guerre

Have you forgotten the password already?
The castle is shut and becomes a prison,
The lovely lady on the battlements sings her song
While the prisoner in solitary moans.
Will you rediscover the path, the plain,
Source and sanctuary in the heart of the forests,
The bend in the river where dawn appeared,
The evening star and the full moon?
A forked serpent springs at man,
Entwining him, binding him in its coils,
The lady sighs on the edge of the battlements,
The setting sun glitters on the spears.
Time never to return springs at man,
Entwining him, binding him in its years.
Loves! Seasons! Faded beauties!
Serpents coiled in the underbrush.

État de veille

THE WATCHMAN OF
THE PONT-AU-CHANGE

I am the watchman of the rue de Flandre.
I watch while Paris sleeps.
Far to the north, fire lights up the night sky.
I hear planes flying over the city.

I am the watchman of the Point du Jour.
The Seine winds along in the darkness around the Auteuil Viaduct,
Under twenty-three bridges across Paris.
I hear bombs exploding to the west.

I am the watchman of the Porte Dorée.
Shadows of the Vincennes forest thicken around the castle.
I have heard cries from the direction of Creteil
And trains rolling east in a wave of defiant song.

I am the watchman of the Poterne des Peupliers.
The south wind brings me acrid smoke,
Vague murmurs and sounds of the dying
Which fade away in Plaisance or Vaugirard.

To the north, to the south, to east and west,
Nothing but the thunder of war converging on Paris.
I am the watchman of the Pont-au-Change
Awake in the heart of Paris in the growing roar
And I recognize the panicked nightmares of the enemy,
The victory shouts of the allies and the French,
The agonized screams of our brothers tortured by Hitler's Germans.

I am the watchman of the Pont-au-Change
Watching not only this night over Paris,
This stormy night not only over Paris in her fever and exhaustion,
But over the whole world which surrounds and crushes us.

In the crisp air all the sounds of war

Converge on this place where men have lived so long.

Cries, songs, sounds of the dying, sounds of riot, they come from
    everywhere.
Victory, suffering and death, a sky the color of white wine and tea.
From the four corners of the horizon, across the barriers of earth,
With the scent of vanilla, of wet earth and blood,
Of saltwater, with powder and funeral fires,
With kisses from an unknown giant sinking at each step into earth
    slippery with human flesh.

I am the watchman of the Pont-au-Change
And I greet you on the threshold of the promised day,
All you my comrades from the rue de Flandre to the Poterne des
    Peupliers,
From Point du Jour to Porte Dorée.

I greet you who sleep
After your dangerous secret work,
Printers, bomb-carriers, railyard-wreckers, incendiaries,
Distributors of tracts, smugglers, messengers,
I greet you who resist, twenty-year-olds with smiles as pure as springs,
Old men more venerable than bridges, strong men, images
    of the seasons,
I greet you on the threshold of the new morning.

I greet you on the banks of the Thames,
Comrades of all nations present at the meeting,
In the ancient English capital,
In ancient London, in ancient Britain.

Americans of all races and flags,
Beyond the broad Atlantic,
From Canada to Mexico, from Brazil to Cuba,
Comrades from Rio, from Tehuantepec, from New York and San
    Francisco.

I have made a rendezvous with the whole earth on the
        Pont-au-Change,
Watching and fighting like you. Just now,
Warned by his heavy, ringing footsteps,
I too have slaughtered my enemy.

He is dead in the gutter, this nameless Hitler German,
His face soiled with mud, his memory already rotting.
While I heard your voices from the four seasons,
Friends, friends and brothers of friendly nations.
I heard your voices in the scent of African orange trees,
In the heavy staleness of the Pacific,
White squadrons of hands held out in the darkness,
Men of Algiers, Honolulu, Chungking,
Men of Fez, of Dakar, of Ajaccio.

Terrifying, unnerving clamor, rhythms of lungs and hearts,
From the Russian front blazing in the snow,
From Lake Ilmen to Kiev, from the Dnieper to Pripet,
You come to me, born from millions of breasts.

I hear you and understand you, Norwegians, Danes, Hollanders,
Belgians, Czechs, Poles, Greeks, Luxemburgers,
Albanians and Yugoslavs, comrades of battle,
I hear your voices and I call to you,
I call to you in a language known to all
A language that has only one word:
Freedom!

And I tell you I am watching and I have slaughtered one of Hitler's
        men.
He is dead in the empty street.
In the heart of the unmoved city I have avenged my brothers
        assassinated
At the fort at Romainville and on Mt. Valerien,
In the fleeting reborn echoes of the world, the city, and the seasons.

And others like me watch and kill,
Like me they lie in wait for ringing footsteps in deserted streets,
Like me they hear the chaos and the thunder of earth.

For the earth is a camp lighted by thousands of fires.
On the eve of battle, watch is kept throughout the earth
And perhaps, comrades, you hear the voices,
Voices that come from here when night falls,
That tear at lips hungry for kisses
That fly endlessly across great stretches
Like migratory birds blinded by beacon lights
Smashing themselves against the fiery windows.

Let my voice come to you
Warm, joyful, and determined,
Without fear and without remorse,
Let my voice come to you with that of my comrades,
The voice of ambush and the French vanguard.

Listen to us in your turn, sailors, pilots, soldiers,
We wish you good morning
We speak to you not of our suffering but of our hope,
On the threshold of the new day we wish you good morning.

To you who are near and, also, to you
Who will receive our morning prayer
At the moment when the early dawn enters your houses in straw boots.
Good morning just the same and good morning for tomorrow!
Good morning with full heart and with all our being!
Good morning, good morning, the sun is going to rise over Paris,
Even if the clouds hide it it will be there,
Good morning, good morning, with all my heart good morning!

L'Honneur des poètes, II published under the name Valentin Guillois

What sort of arrow split the sky and this rock?
It quivers, spreading like a peacock's fan
Like the mist around the shaft and knotless feathers
Of a comet come to nest at midnight.

How blood surges from the gaping wound,
Lips already silencing the murmur and the cry,
One solemn finger holds back time, confusing
The witness of the eyes where the deed is written.

Silence? We still know the passwords.
Lost sentinels far from the watch fires
We smell the odor of honeysuckle and surf
Rising in the dark shadows.

Distance, let dawn leap the void at last,
And a single beam of light make a rainbow on the water
Its quiver full of reeds,
Sign of the return of archers and patriotic songs.

Contrée

March 28
and
July 15, 1944

My love,

Our suffering would be unbearable if we couldn't think of it as a passing and sentimental illness. Our rediscoveries will adorn our life for at least thirty years. As for me, I'm taking a deep drink of youth, and I'll come back to you full of love and strength! During our separation a birthday, mine, was the occasion of a long fantasy about you. Will my letter reach you in time for your birthday? I would've liked to give you 100,000 American cigarettes, a dozen dresses from the great couturiers, an apartment on the rue Seine, a car, the cottage in the Compiègne forest, the one on Belle-Isle and a little four-sous bouquet. While I'm gone, keep flowers around all the time; I'll pay you back for them. All the rest, I promise it to you later.

But above all else, drink a bottle of good wine and think of me. I hope our friends won't forget to visit you that day. I thank them for their courage and devotion. About a week ago I got a package from J-L Barrault. Kiss him for me, and Madeleine Renaud too; the package is proof my letter got through. I haven't gotten an answer; I'm waiting for one every day. Kiss everyone in the family, Lucienne, Aunt Juliet, Georges. If you run into Passeur's brother, give him my best and ask him if he knows anyone who can help you if you need it. What's happening with my books at the printer's? I've got a lot of ideas for poems and novels. I regret not having the freedom or the time to write them. But you can tell Gallimard that within three months after I get back he'll have the manuscript of a love story in an entirely new genre. I'm ending this letter for today.

Today, July 15th, I got four letters, from Barrault, Julia, Dr. Benet, and Daniel. Thank them and apologize for me for not answering. I'm allowed only one letter a month. Still no word from you, but they send me news of you; that will be for the next time. I hope that letter is our life to come. My love, I embrace you as tenderly as propriety allows in a letter which has to pass the censor. A thousand kisses. Have you gotten the little trunk I sent to the hotel in Compiègne?

Robert

Buchenwald

Chorus (hurried and overlapping):

    Chalk and flint and grass and chalk and flint

    And flint and dust and chalk and flint

    Grass, grass and flint and chalk, flint and chalk

        (slowing)

    Flint, flint and chalk

    And chalk and flint

    And chalk . . .

A voice:

    Somewhere between l'Hay-les-Roses

    And Bourg-la-Reine and Anthony

    Between the roses of l'Hay

    Between Clamart and Anthony

Chorus (very rhythmical):

    Chalk and flint—chalk and flint

    And chalk

    And flint and chalk and flint and chalk

    And flint

A voice:

    Between the roses of l'Hay

    And the trees of Clamart

    Have you seen the siren

    The siren of Anthony

    Who sang in Bourg-la-Reine

    Who sings yet in Fresnes.

Chorus:

    Soil of Compiègne!

    Rich yet barren earth

    Earth of flint and chalk

    We make footprints in your flesh

    So that someday the spring rain

    May lie there like the eye of a bird

    And reflect the sky, the sky above Compiègne

174

With your images and stars
Heavy with memory and dream
Harder than flint
More yielding than chalk under a knife
A voice:
In Paris near Bourg-la-Reine
I left my loves alone
Ah! may the sirens lull them
I sleep tranquil, o my loves
And at l'Hay I gather roses
That I will one day bring you
Heavy with perfume and dream
And, like your eyelids, opened
To the bright sun of a somewhat longer life
Filled with flashes of lightning like flintstone,
Luminous like chalk.
Chorus (staggered):
And chalk and flint and flint and chalk
Soil of Compiègne!
Soil made for walking
And the long stand of trees,
Soil of Compiègne!
Like all the soil of earth,
Soil of Compiègne!
One day we will shake our dust off
Onto your dust
And leave singing.
A voice:
We will leave singing
Singing to our loves
Life is short and short the time.
Second voice:
Nothing is more beautiful than our loves.
Another voice:
We will leave our dust
In the dust of Compiègne

(emphasizing each syllable):
And we will carry off our loves
Our loves may we remember them
Chorus:
May we remember them.

Choix de poèmes (1946) Valentin Guillois

EPITAPH

I lived in these times and I've been dead
A thousand years. I lived, not fallen but hunted.
With all human nobility imprisoned,
I was free among the masked slaves.

I lived in these times yet I was free.
I watched the river the earth and sky
Revolve around me, keeping their balance,
The seasons bringing birds and honey.

You who are living, what have you done with these treasures?
Do you regret the time of my struggle?
Have you raised your crops for a common harvest?
Have you made my town a richer place?

Living men, have no fear of me, for I am dead.
Nothing is left of my spirit or my body.

Contrée

There is a poetic constant. There are changes of fashion. There are changes of fad. There are also themes so overbearing they must be expressed at any cost. These themes exist at this moment and must be expressed at this moment.

Each person finds his poetic food where he likes. Reading *Dieux Verts* by Pierre Devaux has taught me more about a possible poetic technique than such and such a weighty essay.

Villon, Gerard de Nerval, Gongora, together with the great Baffo, seem to me subjects for current reflections concerning poetic technique. To wed common language, the most common, to an indescribable atmosphere, to sharp imagery; to annex domains which, even in our day, seem incompatible with that fiendish "noble language" which is endlessly reborn in languages ripped away from the mangy Cerberus which guards the entrance to the poetic domain, is what seems to me the work worth doing, without forgetting, I repeat, certain overbearing themes of inspiration of the moment. . . .

The greatest names of our time (I am speaking of poets) are still not assured of a prominent place on the third shelf of an inquisitive scholar of the year 2000. However, that isn't important. It may be that great poetry is necessarily of the present, from events . . . therefore it may be short-lived.

Poetry may be this or it may be that. But it shouldn't necessarily be this or that . . . except delirious and lucid.

Schools follow and get mixed up with each other. Romanticism now comprises the Parnassian school, symbolism, naturalism. There is an atheistic Romanticism, a Catholic Romanticism. And, looked at closely, Romanticism reconciles the philosophical eighteenth century and the metaphysical Middle Ages . . . like the cook making a salad who thought he could reconcile oil and vinegar.

It seems to me that beyond Surrealism there is something very mysterious to be dealt with, that beyond automatism there is the intentional, that beyond poetry there is the poem, that beyond poetry received there is poetry imposed, that beyond free poetry there is the free poet.

I feel that mysterious domain I just spoke of behind Nerval, whom it will be necessary to start out from again in order to be liberated from Mallarmé, Rimbaud and Lautreamont. Though perhaps the doors to this domain can only be opened with a word from the jargon ballads of Villon.

Gongora . . . the poem follows its perfectly straight path on a wide avenue across the dark, tufted forest; though to both left and right, little intersecting roads lead away, sinuous paths toward the edges, and Gongora doesn't leave that out, he keeps it, he absorbs it, he takes it away like an escaped convict who'd take the fields with him instead of taking to them.

Paris, January 1944

COMING DOWN HILLSIDES
IN SPRING

Coming down hillsides in the spring
At the time of day when dew glistens on the spiderwebs
In the faraway sound of iron hammered in a forge
In the reflection of light on the river.

Coming down hillsides in the spring
I tell you I've left shame and bitterness with the winter
A deep love overwhelms me with joy
And even my hatred overwhelms and elates me.

Coming down hillsides in the spring
Abandoning worm-eaten graves and memories
Drunk on the sweet odors of earth and air
Opening myself up to take in the whole world.

Coming down hillsides in the spring,
I have broken the scales I weighed life and death in,
Finally ready to welcome summer and the harvest-time,
Ready to accept the interruption of my journey.

Coming down hillsides in the spring
Living with greater joy than in the days of my youth,
But conscious of the sweet odors of earth and air
Of the echo of a little faraway song
Sung in a quavering voice by a little girl
I will never know.

Sens

THE PROPHECY

From a square in Paris such a clear spring will gush
That the blood of virgins and glacier streams
Will seem opaque beside it.
The stars will come in swarms from their faraway hives
And cluster to gaze at their reflections
   near the Tour St. Jacques.

From a square in Paris such a clear spring will gush
That some will go there at dawn to bathe in secret.
St. Opportune and her washerwomen will be its godmothers
And it will flow from north to south.

A big red chestnut tree is growing in the square
Where the spring-to-be will flow.
Perhaps in my old age
I'll hear it murmuring;

For the song of that clear spring is so sweet
It already bathes my eyes and my heart.
It will be the most beautiful tributary of the Seine,
The surest proof of springtime to come,
   their birds and their flowers.

Contrée

Carolyn Forché's first book of poetry, *Gathering the Tribes* (Yale University Press), won the Yale Series of Younger Poets Award in 1976. Her second collection, *The Country Between Us* (Harper and Row Publishers, Inc.), was the 1981 Lamont Selection of the Academy of American Poets. She was a recipient of a Lannan Foundation Fellowship in 1990, and currently teaches at George Mason University in Virginia.

William Kulik was born in Newark, New Jersey, in 1937. Hunter, gardener, fisherman and cartoonist, he lives in Philadelphia with his wife, Catharine, and their two children, Amy and Alexander. His first volume of Robert Desnos translations, *The Voice,* was published by Mushinsha in 1971; his latest, a translation of Desnos's last book, *Contrée,* will be published by the Windhover Press. Currently he is working on translation of *L'Enfant,* a novel by Jules Valles, and *The Selected Poems of Tristan Tzara.* He teaches English at Community College of Philadelphia.